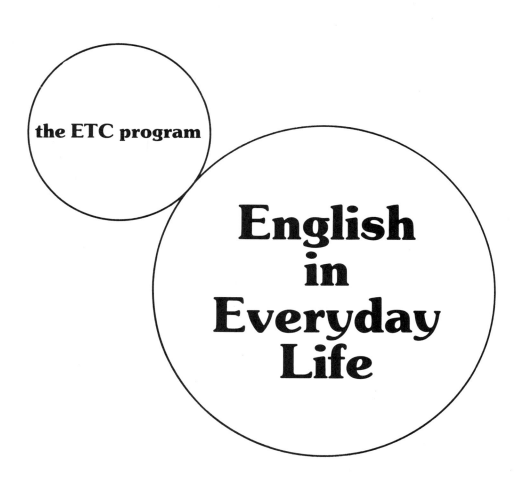

the ETC program

English in Everyday Life

A Competency-Based Reading/Writing Book

Elaine Kirn
West Los Angeles College

McGraw-Hill, Inc.
New York St. Louis San Francisco Auckland Bogotá
Caracas Lisbon London Madrid Mexico Milan
Montreal New Delhi Paris San Juan Singapore
Sydney Tokyo Toronto

This is an  book.

English in Everyday Life
A Competency-Based Reading/Writing Book

5 6 7 8 9 0 MAL MAL 9 5 4 3 2

ISBN 0-07-553757-5 (Student Edition)
ISBN 0-07-554239-0 (Instructor's Edition)

Library of Congress Cataloging-in Publication Data

Kirn, Elaine.
   The *ETC* program. English in everyday life : a competency-based reading/writing book / Elaine Kirn.
      p.   cm.
   Level 2.
   1. English language—Textbooks for foreign speakers.
2. Reading (Adult education). I. Title.
PE1128.K4795   1988   428.6′4   87-37629

This book was set in Century Schoolbook by Etcetera Graphics.
The project manager was Marian Hartsough.
Series design and production was done by Etcetera Graphics.
Cover designer was Juan Vargas, Vargas/Williams Design.
Illustrations were done by Terry Wilson.
The production supervisor was Cathy Miller.
Malloy Lithographing was printer and binder.

Contents

Preface

Language is me.
Language is you.
Language is people.
Language is what people do.
Language is loving and hurting.
Language is clothes, faces, gestures, responses.
Language is imagining, designing, creating, destroying.
Language is control and persuasion.
Language is communication.
Language is laughter.
Language is growth.
Language is me.
The limits of my language are the limits of my world.

And you can't package *that* up in a book, can you?

—New Zealand Curriculum Development

No, you can't package language in a book or even a whole program of books, but you have to start somewhere.

About the *ETC* Program

ETC is a six-level ESL (English as a second language) program for adults who are learning English to improve their lives and work skills. The material of this level is divided into three books, carefully coordinated, chapter by chapter, in theme, competency goals, grammar, and vocabulary. For a representation of the scope and sequence of the program, see the back cover of any volume.

ETC has been designed for maximum efficiency and flexibility. To choose the materials most suitable for your particular teaching situation, decide on the appropriate level by assessing the ability and needs of the students you expect to be teaching. The competency descriptions included in each instructor's manual ("About This Level") will aid you in your assessment.

About This Book

ETC English in Everyday Life: A Competency-Based Reading/Writing Book offers a large variety of simplified "realia"—forms, ads, signs, letters, schedules, and other examples of the reading material that ESL students encounter daily.

The writing material offers practice in the kinds of writing tasks that students encounter in everyday life—filling out forms; writing lists, notes, and messages; and the like. Although most of the writing activities provide clear guidelines, they are designed to help students develop the practical writing skills necessary for work and daily life.

Organization

Like most other books in the *ETC* program, the reading/writing book consists of an introduction and ten chapters, each divided into four parts with specific purposes.

- *Part One: Read and Understand* presents simplified realia and exercises, sometimes preceded by reading selections with practical and cultural information.

- *Part Two: Information* continues with more specific kinds of realia for students to interpret and related practical writing tasks.

- *Part Three: Spelling* concentrates on sound-symbol correspondences (phonics) and spelling rules.

- *Part Four: Read and Write* points out writing rules and conventions, gives examples, and provides controlled writing practice.

Symbols

The following symbols appear throughout the text:

    ✱   a challenging activity designed for more advanced students

    ✱✱   a "beyond-the-text" activity

Available Ancillaries

The instructor's manual for this text includes:

- a general introduction to the *ETC* program, this level, and this book

- general suggestions for teaching techniques to use in presenting the various kinds of activities

- an answer key for all text exercises

- progress tests, one to accompany each chapter of the text, that can be duplicated and distributed to students

- an answer key for the progress tests

Acknowledgments

To Etcetera, ETC, ETC, because we finally did it.

Appreciation beyond frustration goes to the many class testers and reviewers, reviewers, reviewers—whose opinions lie at the core of the *ETC* program. Thanks to the following reviewers, whose comments both favorable and critical, were of great value in the development of *ETC English in Everyday Life*:

Peter T. Bomba, Carol Cargill-Vroman, Nancy Frothingham, Alice Gosak,
Julia Jolly, Nick Kremer, Carolyn McCarthy, Maryann O'Brien, Nancy Olds,
Kara Rosenberg, Edward Schiffer, Margaret Segal, Jane Sturtevant,
Kent Sutherland, Elizabeth Templin, Mary Thurber, Jane Turner,
Stephanie Vandrick, Julia Villaseñor, Betsey Warrick, Patricia K. Werner,
Roni R. Wong, Synthia Woodcock.

The author wishes to thank the staff at Random House:
- Eirik Borve and Karen Judd—for keeping promises,
- Lesley Walsh—for being as efficient as ever,
- Marian Hartsough—for communicating where need be, and
- Edith Brady, Cynthia Ward, and the sales staff—for what is yet to come.

Heartfelt thanks to the staff and supporters of Etcetera Graphics, Canoga Park, California:
- Susan Smith Amatori—for copyediting and typemarking,
- Terry Wilson—for his inspired artwork and patience,
- Cindra Tardif—for expert typesetting, and
- Sheila Clark—for alert and patient production,

and gratitude, appreciation, and love to
- Anthony Thorne-Booth—for his management, expertise, and hard work,
- Karol Roff—for helping, helping, helping,
- Sally Kostal—for jumping in to rescue us and to keep us calm,
- Chuck Alessio—for everything and more

and to Andi Kirn—for putting up with it all.

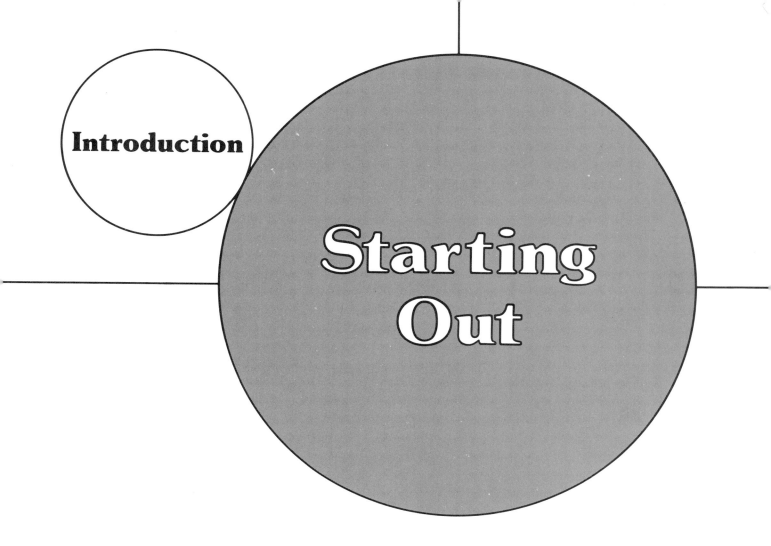

Introduction

Starting Out

COMPETENCIES: Using letters and numbers
Recognizing the names of people and countries

LETTERS AND NUMBERS

1.

2.

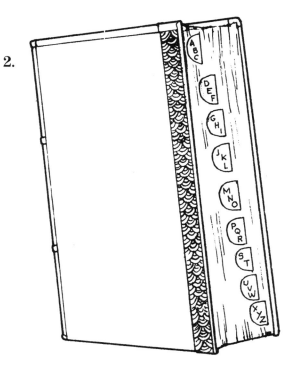

3.

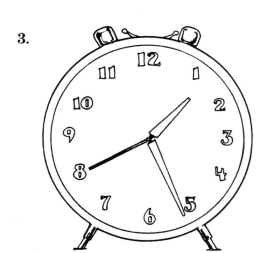

4.

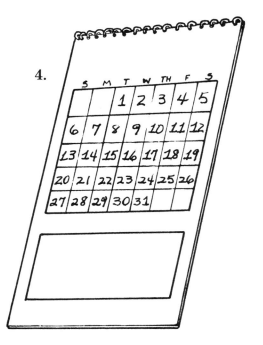

THE LETTERS OF THE ALPHABET

PRINTING

A B C D E F G H I J K L M

small   a b c d e f g h i j k l m

HANDWRITING

capital   *A B C D E F G H I J K L M*

small   *a b c d e f g h i j k l m*

PRINTING

capital   N O P Q R S T U V W X Y Z

small   n o p q r s t u v w x y z

HANDWRITING

capital   *N O P Q R S T U V W X Y Z*

small   *n o p q r s t u v w x y z*

A. Draw a circle.

1. A a (E) 𝒶 a
2. B (d) b 𝐵 𝒷
3. C c c 𝒞 𝒶
4. D 𝒪 𝒹 d 𝒟
5. F E 𝑒 e 𝓔
6. F 𝓕 f 𝒻 𝓔
7. g 𝑔 G 𝑔 𝒢
8. h 𝒽 𝓗 𝒷 H
9. 𝓁 I 𝒾 i 𝓘

10. J j y 𝒿 𝒿
11. K 𝓀 b k 𝒦
12. l 𝓁 𝓛 𝓁 L
13. m 𝓂 M W 𝓂
14. n m 𝓃 𝒩 N
15. Q O 𝑜 o 𝒪
16. P 𝒫 p 𝓡 𝓅
17. Q 𝓆 𝓅 q 𝒬
18. r 𝓈 𝓡 R 𝓇

19. S 𝓈 𝒮 s c
20. T I 𝒯 t 𝓉
21. O U 𝒰 𝓊 u
22. u 𝓋 v 𝒱 V
23. w 𝒲 𝒱 W 𝓌
24. X 𝓍 x 𝒳 v
25. g y 𝒴 Y 𝓎
26. z 𝓏 s 𝓏 Z

B. Print and use handwriting.

A	a	*A*	*a*	B					c		
		D						*e*	F		
		g				*H*					*i*
J				k					*L*		
		m	N						o		
		P					*q*	R			
	s					*T*					*u*
V				w					*X*		
		y	Z								

read	*read*	draw	
name			*last*
	first	study	
write			*words*
	print	small	
letter			*number*
	middle	circle.	

The Names of People

First	Middle	Last		Last	First	Middle
James	Lee	Smith		Smith,	James	Lee
Juan	Carlos	Flores		Flores,	Juan	Carlos
Wan-Chun		Yang		Yang,	Wan-Chun	
Mary	Kay	Watt-Jones		Watt-Jones,	Mary	Kay

C. Print and sign your name in the books of your classmates.

1. _____ , _____   _____
       LAST   FIRST   MIDDLE

   _____
       SIGNATURE

2. _____ , _____   _____
       LAST   FIRST   MIDDLE

   _____
       SIGNATURE

3. _____ , _____   _____
       LAST   FIRST   MIDDLE

   _____
       SIGNATURE

4. _____ , _____   _____
       LAST   FIRST   MIDDLE

   _____
       SIGNATURE

5. _____ , _____   _____
       LAST   FIRST   MIDDLE

   _____
       SIGNATURE

D. Add more names of countries.

THE NAMES OF COUNTRIES

North America

Canada
Mexico

_____

Central America

El Salvador
Nicaragua
Costa Rica

_____

_____

_____

South America

Brazil
Venezuela
Argentina

_____

_____

_____

Europe

England
West Germany
France
Poland

_____

_____

_____

The Middle East

Saudi Arabia
Iran
Israel

_____

_____

_____

Asia

China
Japan
South Korea

_____

_____

_____

Africa

Egypt
Ethiopia
Nigeria

_____

_____

_____

_____ **E.** **Write the names of countries on the maps.**

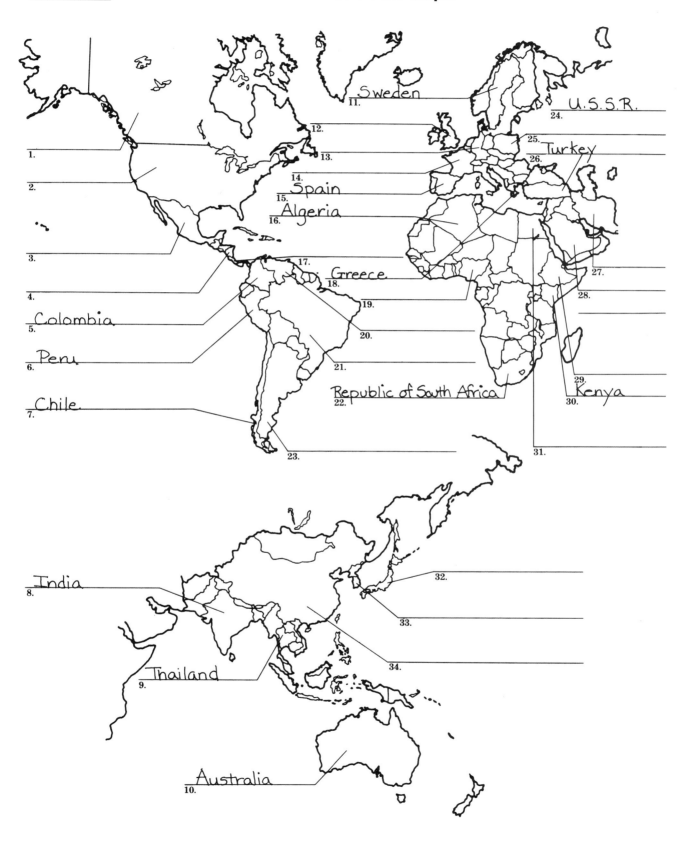

11. Sweden
1.
2.
3.
4.
5. Colombia
6. Peru
7. Chile
8. India
9. Thailand
10. Australia
12.
13.
14.
15. Spain
16. Algeria
17.
18. Greece
19.
20.
21.
22. Republic of South Africa
23.
24. U.S.S.R.
25.
26. Turkey
27.
28.
29.
30. Kenya
31.
32.
33.
34.

F.   Read and write the numbers.

The Numbers 1–100

1		3				7		9	
		13					18		
								49	
	52								
		63		65					
			74						
		83							
81									
	92					97		99	

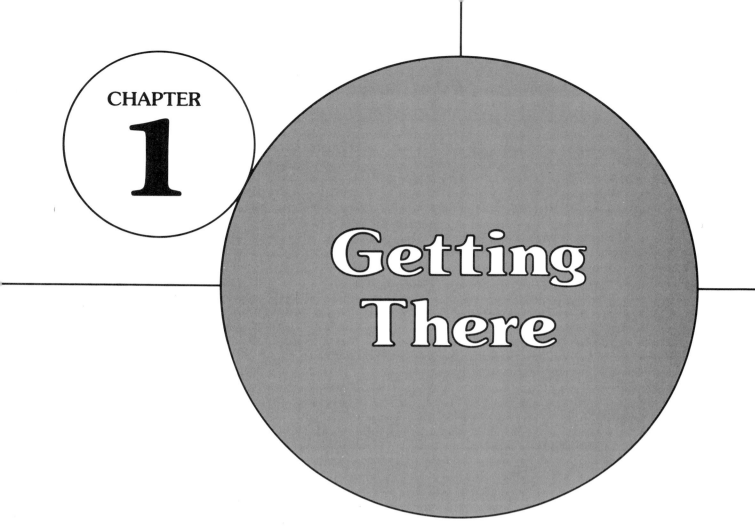

CHAPTER 1

Getting There

COMPETENCIES: Understanding instructions and street signs
Reading and writing addresses
Understanding maps and street directions

SPELLING: The vowels *a, e, i, o, u*

GRAMMAR FOCUS: The imperative
Can/can't

PART ONE / READ AND UNDERSTAND

● Instructions and Street Signs

Study at the English Language Center

Learn in
small classes.

Meet students
from many
countries.

Understand and
speak English.
Read and write.

Call today.
Don't wait
another day.

How to Get There

The downtown
English Language Center
is on the corner of
Grand Avenue and Flower Street.

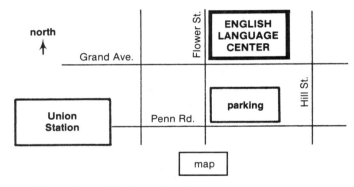

north

Grand Ave.

Flower St.

ENGLISH LANGUAGE CENTER

Hill St.

Union Station

Penn Rd.

parking

map

— You can take the train to Union Station. Then walk two blocks to the school.

— You can take Bus 7 downtown. Get off at Grand Avenue and Hill Street. Go one block west to the school.

— You can drive to the ELC. Don't park on the street. The school parking lot is on the corner of Penn Road and Flower Street.

A. Answer the questions. Write *yes* or *no*.

1. _yes_ Can students learn English at the English Language Center?

2. _yes_ Is the ELC a school downtown?

3. _____ Is it on the corner of Penn Road and Union Avenue?

4. _____ Can students walk from the train station to the school?

5. _____ Can they get off Bus 7 on Center Boulevard and cross the street to the ELC?

6. _____ Can they drive to the school and park in a lot?

B. On the lines, write the letters of the signs.

1. _E_ Don't make a U-turn.

2. ____ Wait for the bus here.

3. ____ You can't turn left.

4. ____ You can drive in here.

5. ____ You can't drive into this street.

6. ____ Watch for children.

7. ____ Drive out here.

8. ____ Don't park here.

9. ____ Don't cross the street now.

10. ____ You can drive 25 miles an hour.

*C. Look at signs on the street. Write the words. In English class, talk about the signs.

PART TWO / INFORMATION

● Addresses, Telephone Numbers, and Times

Addresses			Telephone Numbers		
number	street	apartment or office	area code	local number	extension
8094	Park Avenue	#102	(619)	555-2610	Ext. 387
eighty ninety-four		number one- oh-two	six-one- nine	five-five-five two-six-one-oh	three-eight- seven

Times				
7:00	5:36	10:20	-	1:30
seven o' clock	five thirty-six	ten twenty	to	one thirty

A. On the lines, write the information from the picture on page 12.

	Addresses	Telephone Numbers
1. The Grand Hotel	_1111 Grand Avenue._	_____
2. The Grand Book Store	_____	_____
3. A drugstore	_____	_____
4. The Elm Place Hotel	_____	_____
5. The office of the Computer Learning School	_____	_____
6. Information about English classes	_____	_____
7. An apartment for rent	_____	_____

Times

8. The Computer Learning School office is open from _____ to _____ .

9. The gas station is open from _____ to _____ .

10. The time in the picture is _____ .

Abbreviations in Addresses

You can write abbreviations in addresses. These are short forms of names.

Examples   St. = Street   Rd. = Road

B. Write the abbreviations on the lines.

St.	Ave.	Blvd.	Rd.	Dr.	Pl.	Ct.	Apt.

1. _Ave._
   Avenue

2. _____
   Street

3. _____
   Drive

4. _____
   Place

5. _____
   Road

6. _____
   Court

7. _____
   Boulevard

8. _____
   Apartment

_____ **C.** **Read the card. Write the information on the lines.**

```
                    CLASS ENROLLMENT CARD

NAME  Gomez      Martin        TELEPHONE  (415) 555-2450
       last        first                  area code    number

ADDRESS  201          Crest Road            42
          number         street           apartment

CLASSROOM  14    TIME  2:00     Martin Gomez
                                           signature
```

1. last name _Gomez_____ first name _____

2. number _____ street _____ apartment _____

3. area code _____ local telephone number _____

4. room number _____ time of the class _____

_____ **D.** **Print the information about you. Write your signature.**

```
                    CLASS ENROLLMENT CARD

NAME  _____   TELEPHONE  _____
        last        first                    area code    number

ADDRESS  _____
            number         street           apartment

CLASSROOM  _____  TIME  _____  _____
                                              signature
```

_____ ***E.** **Get enrollment cards or forms from your school. Read them in
English class. Talk about the information. Fill out the cards.**

PART THREE / SPELLING

● The Vowels a, e, i, o, u

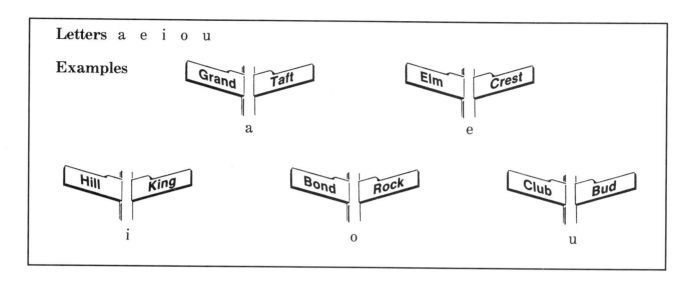

Letters a e i o u

Examples

Grand | Taft   a

Elm | Crest   e

Hill | King   i

Bond | Rock   o

Club | Bud   u

___ **A.** **Listen to the words. Write the vowel letters.**   a e i o u

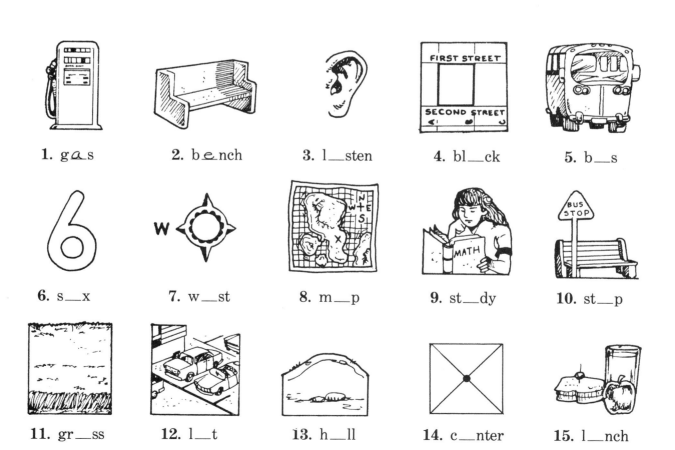

1. g a s

2. b e nch

3. l__sten

4. bl__ck

5. b__s

6. s__x

7. w__st

8. m__p

9. st__dy

10. st__p

11. gr__ss

12. l__t

13. h__ll

14. c__nter

15. l__nch

_____ B. Listen to the story. Write the vowel letters.

1. | a |

Oh, no.

No g⌣s.

2. | a o u i |

Eight bl⌣cks to the b__s st__p __t

N__sh Dr__ve and Cl__b Street.

3. | a e i | Don't st__nd on

the gr__ss. S__t

on the b__nch.

4. | a e u |

G__t on b__s number t__n

__t l:06. Go w__est.

5. | a e i o |

P__ss H__ll and B__nd.

K__ng Place __s n__xt.

Gr__nd Avenue.

6. | a e u |

G__t off at the English L__nguage

C__nter. R__n to cl__ss.

_____ C. Now read the above words and story aloud.

_____ *D. Write other words with one vowel letter (*a, e, i, o, u*). Pronounce them. Tell the meanings.

PART FOUR / READ AND WRITE

● Maps ● Street Directions

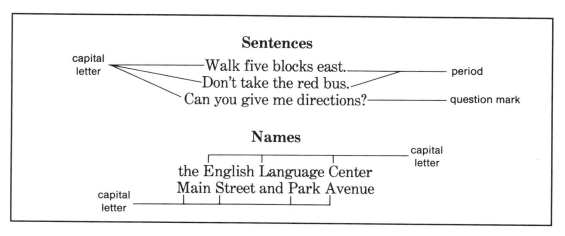

Sentences

capital letter —— Walk five blocks east. —— period
Don't take the red bus.
Can you give me directions? —— question mark

Names

the English Language Center —— capital letter
capital letter —— Main Street and Park Avenue

A. Change small letters to capital letters. Write the periods and question marks.

    C

1. ȼan you give me directions to the ȼomputer ℓearning ȿchool ?

2. walk five blocks east   then turn right   pass main street

3. you can take the bus   go to the bus stop at east avenue and park boulevard

4. can you drive to the school   you can park in the lot on flower street

5. drive on highway 10

    to big bend boulevard

    then go north to penn road

    turn right   then go one

    mile to flower street

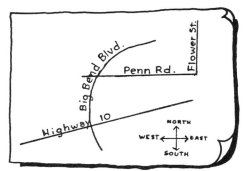

_____ **B.** **Cover the words under each line with paper. Listen and write the sentences. Check your writing. Then draw a line on the map.**

1. _Go north on Penn Avenue._
   Go north on Penn Avenue.

2. _____
   Turn left on King Boulevard.

3. _____
   Walk three blocks to Nash Street.

4. _____
   Turn right. Go one block.

5. _____
   The drugstore is on the corner.

_____ **C.** **Look at the line on the map. Write the directions to the bus station.**

Go one block north on Crest Road.

_____

_____

_____ **D.** **Write directions to a place on the map. Exchange books with another student. Draw a line on the map from the directions.**

_____

_____

_____

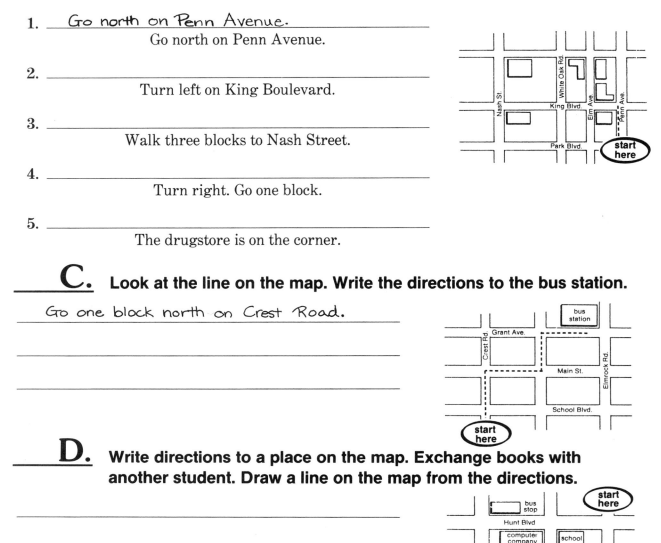

_____ ***E.** **Use maps of your city. Write directions from your school to other places. Exchange maps and directions. Draw lines on the maps from the directions.**

_____ ****F.** **Draw a map from your school to your home. Write directions on another piece of paper. Then work together. Exchange directions. Read them and draw another map. Then compare maps.**

CHAPTER

2

Problems and Solutions

COMPETENCIES: Understanding directories, bulletin boards, and signs
Expressing times and dates
Reading and writing short notes

SPELLING: The vowels *a-e, e-e, i-e, o-e, u-e* (final silent *e*)
Contrast to the spellings *a, e, i, o, u*

GRAMMAR FOCUS: The present tense

PART ONE / READ AND UNDERSTAND

● Directories ● Bulletin Boards ● Signs

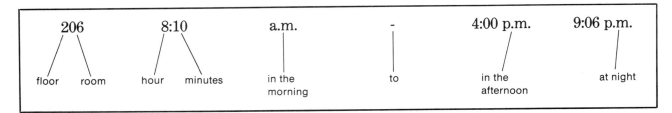

English Language Center
School Directory

bookstore .... basement		housing board 104	
cafeteria .... basement		library 212	
language laboratory ... 210		main office 104	
classrooms .... 3rd floor		restrooms	
information 104		men 110 310	
		women 111 311	

Hours

office .... 9:00 a.m.-4:00 p.m.	library.......... 1:00-8:15 p.m.
cafeteria .... 8:15 a.m.-8:45 p.m.	bookstore .... 9:15-11:45 a.m.

A. On the lines, write the information from the directory.

1. The bookstore and the cafeteria are in the <u>basement</u> .

2. The language laboratory is in Room _____ .

3. In Room 104 you can get _____ and look for _____ .

   It's the main _____ . It's open from 9:00 a.m. to _____ .

4. Room 212 is the _____ . It's open from _____

   to _____ .

5. The restroom are on floors _____ and _____ .

English Language Center Bulletin Board

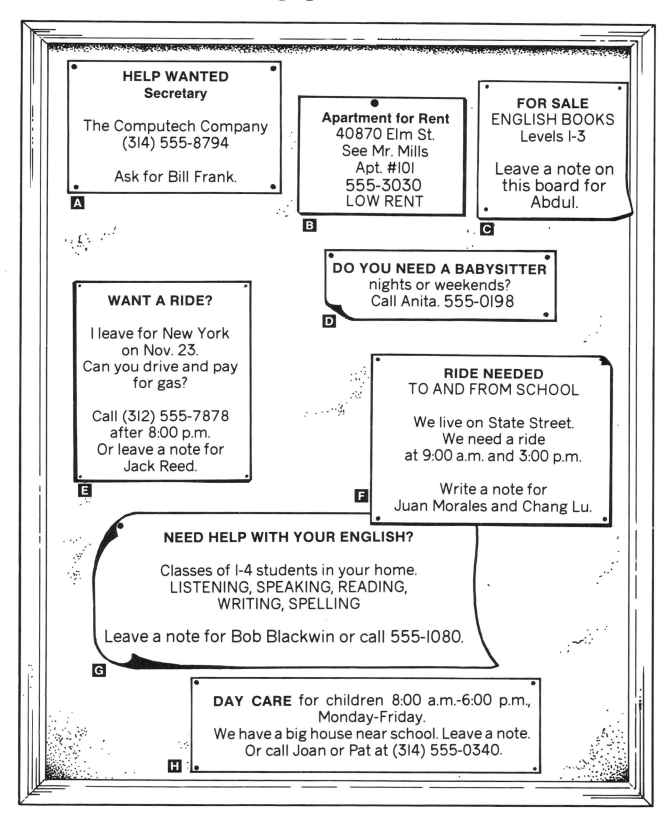

HELP WANTED
Secretary

The Computech Company
(314) 555-8794

Ask for Bill Frank.

A

Apartment for Rent
40870 Elm St.
See Mr. Mills
Apt. #101
555-3030
LOW RENT

B

FOR SALE
ENGLISH BOOKS
Levels 1-3

Leave a note on
this board for
Abdul.

C

DO YOU NEED A BABYSITTER
nights or weekends?
Call Anita. 555-0198

D

WANT A RIDE?

I leave for New York
on Nov. 23.
Can you drive and pay
for gas?

Call (312) 555-7878
after 8:00 p.m.
Or leave a note for
Jack Reed.

E

RIDE NEEDED
TO AND FROM SCHOOL

We live on State Street.
We need a ride
at 9:00 a.m. and 3:00 p.m.

Write a note for
Juan Morales and Chang Lu.

F

NEED HELP WITH YOUR ENGLISH?

Classes of 1-4 students in your home.
LISTENING, SPEAKING, READING,
WRITING, SPELLING

Leave a note for Bob Blackwin or call 555-1080.

G

DAY CARE for children 8:00 a.m.-6:00 p.m.,
Monday-Friday.
We have a big house near school. Leave a note.
Or call Joan or Pat at (314) 555-0340.

H

B. Read the problems. On the lines, write the letters from the notes on the bulletin board on page 21.

1. __H__ You have two small children. You work all morning.
   You go to school in the afternoon.

2. _____ Your friends live in New York. You have time for a trip.
   But you don't have a car.

3. _____ You want a job. You can type. You can answer the telephone.

4. _____ You need books. But you don't want new books.

5. _____ You go to school at night. You have a baby.

6. _____ You need an apartment. You can't pay high rent.

7. _____ You drive to the English Language Center in the morning. You go home in
   the afternoon. You live near State Street. You need money.

8. _____ You take English classes. But you can't understand well. You can't write.
   You can't spell. You need more practice. You have money.

**C. Look at signs in your school. Write the words. In English class, talk about the signs.

PART TWO / INFORMATION

- Dates

JANUARY						
Sunday Sun. **S**	Monday Mon. **M**	Tuesday Tues. **T**	Wednesday Wed. **W**	Thursday Thurs. **T**	Friday Fri. **F**	Saturday Sat. **S**
1 1st first	**2** 2nd second	**3** 3rd third	**4** 4th fourth	**5** 5th fifth	**6** 6th sixth	**7** 7th seventh
8 8th eighth	**9** 9th ninth	**10** 10th tenth	**11** 11th eleventh	**12** 12th twelfth	**13** 13th thirteenth	**14** 14th fourteenth
15 15th fifteenth	**16** 16th sixteenth	**17** 17th seventeenth	**18** 18th eighteenth	**19** 19th nineteenth	**20** 20th twentieth	**21** 21st twenty-first
22 22th twenty-second	**23** 23rd twenty-third	**24** 24th twenty-fourth	**25** 25th twenty-fifth	**26** 26th twenty-sixth	**27** 27th twenty-seventh	**28** 28th twenty-eighth
29 29th twenty-ninth	**30** 30th thirtieth	**31** 31st thirty-first				

A. On the lines, write the information from the calendar.

1. the day of the week of the first day of the month _Sunday_

   the third day _____ the fourteenth day _____

   the twentieth _____ the twenty-fifth _____

2. the dates of the four Fridays in the month _6th_ _____ _____ _____

   of the five Mondays _____ _____ _____ _____ _____

3. the number of days in the month _____ the number of Sundays _____

Abbreviations for Days and Months
You can use abbreviations for days of the week and months of the year.
Examples
Fri. = Friday   Sat. = Saturday   Feb. = February   Nov. = November

---

B. **Read. Write the answers (days and months) in the crossword puzzle.**

DOWN

1. the fourth day of the week
2. the abbreviation for Saturday
3. the 6th month of the year
4. the day after Wednesday
6. the tenth month of the year
7. the month after June
9. the 3rd month of the year
11. the abbreviation for February

ACROSS

2. Sept. = _____
3. the first month of the year
4. Tues. = _____
5. the abbreviation for November
8. the month before September
9. Mon. = _____
10. the 4th month of the year
11. the abbreviation for Friday
12. the month after April

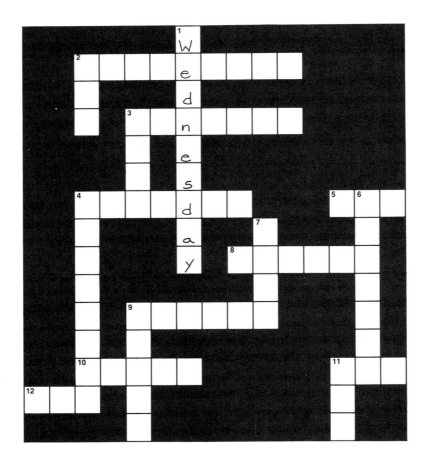

Dates

Sunday, December twenty-first, nineteen sixty-eight =

capital letter—Sun., Dec. 21, 1968

period capital letter period

month   day   year

Dec. 21, 1968 = 12 / 21 / 68

month   day   year

C. Find the same dates. Draw lines.

1. Dec. 1, 1968	6/21/45	**5.** Apr. 2, 1960	9/5/98
2. June 21, 1945	1/8/1898	**6.** Feb. 4, 1960	5/9/89
3. Nov. 11, 1911	11/11/11	**7.** May 9, 1989	4/2/60
4. Jan. 8, 1898	12/1/68	**8.** Sept. 5, 1998	2/4/60

D. Write the dates in another way.

1. Dec. 1, 1968 = _12/1/68_	**6.** 6/28/51 = _____
2. July 18, 1945 = _____	**7.** 2/1/17 = _____
3. Aug. 14, 1888 = _____	**8.** 10/31/94 = _____
4. Mar. 26, 2012 = _____	**9.** 1/12/1845 = _____
5. Nov. 30, 1989 = _____	**10.** 4/22/2031 = _____

E. Write the dates for

1. today _____   4. tomorrow _____

2. next Monday _____   5. your birth _____

3. the first day of your class   6. the last day of your class

_____   _____

PART THREE / SPELLING

● The Vowels *a-e, e-e, i-e, o-e, u-e* ● Contrast to the Spellings *a, e, i, o, u*

Letters	a-e	e-e	i-e	o-e	u-e
Examples	J<u>a</u>n<u>e</u>	P<u>e</u>t<u>e</u>	p<u>i</u>l<u>e</u>	n<u>o</u>t<u>e</u>	t<u>u</u>b<u>e</u>

_____ **A.** **Listen to the words. Write the vowel letters.**   a e i o u

1. p<u>a</u>ge   **2.** h__r__   **3.** t__m__   **4.** h__m__   **5.** J__n__

6. st__r__   **7.** ch__ng__   **8.** t__b__   **9.** th__s__   **10.** r__d__

11. J__n__ and
St__v__ live
h__r__ in
this pl__c__.

12. P__t__ and
G__n__ are
t__r__d.
They can't
dr__v__.

13. J__m__s
and M__k__
are aw__k__
at f__v__
o'clock.

14. Exc__s__
me. When can I
ph__n__? And
please don't
sm__k__.

____ ***B.** **Write other words with _e_ at the end after a consonant (_a-e_, _e-e_, _i-e_, _o-e_, _u-e_). Pronounce them. Tell the meanings.**

Letters	a	e	i	o	u
Examples	J<u>a</u>n	P<u>e</u>t	p<u>i</u>ll	n<u>o</u>t	t<u>u</u>b

____ **C.** **Listen to the words. Write the vowel letters.** 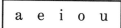 a e i o u

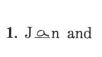

1. J a n and

   J a n e

2. P__t__ with

   his p__t

3. a p__l__

   of p__lls

4. n__t a

   n__t__

5. t__b__ in

   a t__b

____ **D.** **Now read the words and sentences from A and C aloud.**

PART FOUR / READ AND WRITE

● Short Notes

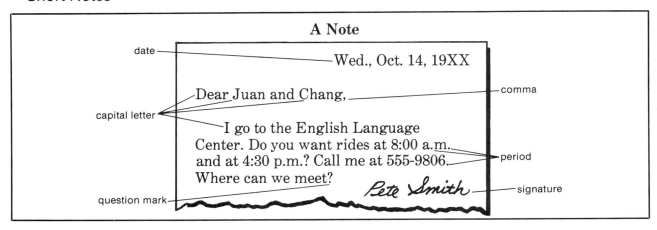

A Note

date ———————————— Wed., Oct. 14, 19XX

Dear Juan and Chang, ——————— comma

capital letter

I go to the English Language
Center. Do you want rides at 8:00 a.m.
and at 4:30 p.m.? Call me at 555-9806. ——— period
Where can we meet?
                                    Pete Smith ——— signature
question mark

A. Write the information from the note.

Two students need a ride to and from school.

1. their names ___Juan, Chang_____

A student can give them a ride.

2. his name _____ his telephone number _____

3. the times for rides _____

4. the date of the note _____

    the day of the week _____

B. Change the small letters to capital letters. Write the punctuation (periods, question marks, and commas).

                                                        nov   2   19XX

D
ɗear   joan   and   pat

   we   have   two   small   children   i   work   in   the   morning   i   go   to

school   in   the   afternoon   i   can't   take   them   with   me   we   need

child   care   all   day   what   do   they   do   at   your   place   can   i   get

them   at   6:30   p   m   call   me   at   555-3421   with   more   information

   thank   you
                                              Emiko Onada

C. **Cover the words under each line with paper. Listen and write. Then check your writing.**

Mon., Nov. 9

Dear Bob,

I need help with English.

When do you teach?   What do I pay?

Can I study at your place?   You can call me

at 555-1221 from 10:30 a.m. to 4:00 p.m. Monday to Friday.

Lee Chen

D. **Look at the notes from a bulletin board. Finish the answers.**

1. the date today

RIDERS WANTED
to New York.
Leave Dec. l6.
Drive.
Pay l/2 gas.

Leave note for
Jack Reed
ll Oak St.

Dear _Jack_ ,
    2. the first name

I need a ride to _____ . I can leave on
               3. the place

_____ . I can drive and pay for gas. Please call me
4. the date

at _____ . You can get me from
    5. your number

_____ to _____ . Thank you.
6. a time   **7.** a time

_____
8. your signature

_____
9. the date today

Dear _____ ,
        10. the first name

I need _____ . Can you meet me at
        11. the things

_____ ? I can be there at _____ on
12. a place   13. a time

_____ , _____ . Call me at
14. a day   15. a date

_____ or leave a note.
16. your number

_____
17. your signature

```
FOR SALE
ENGLISH BOOKS
Levels I-3

Leave a note
on this board
for Abdul.
```

*E. **Write a short answer to another note on the bulletin board on page 21.**

_____

_____

_____

_____

_____

_____

_____

_____

F. **Copy a note from a bulletin board. Write a short answer for it. Tell the class about it.

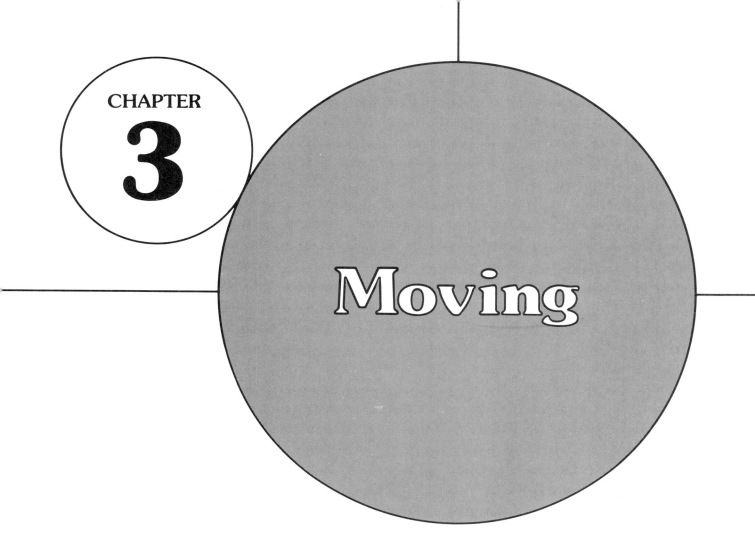

CHAPTER

3

Moving

COMPETENCIES: Understanding housing and sale ads
Reading numbers and amounts of money
Reading and writing names of cities, states,
    provinces; reading zip codes
Understanding and filling out housing
    applications
Reading and writing short letters

SPELLING: The vowels *ai*, *ay*, *ee*, *ea*, *ie*, *oa*, *oo*
Contrast with the spellings *a* (-*e*), *e* (-*e*), *i* (-*e*),
    o (-*e*), *u* (-*e*)

GRAMMAR FOCUS: *There is/are*

PART ONE / READ AND UNDERSTAND

● Housing and Sale Ads

Abbreviations in Newspaper Ads

Newspapers use abbreviations (short forms) in ads.

Examples   furn. = furnished   bedrm. = bedroom   bldg. = building

---

A. Write the words after the abbreviations.

bedroom	apartments	large	utilities	two bedrooms and
building	unfurnished	drapes	carpeting	two bathrooms
dollars	parking	furnished		

1. apts.   =   _apartments_

2. furn.   =   _____

3. crpt.   =   _____

4. bldg.   =   _____

5. lrg.   =   _____

6. 2 + 2   =   _____

7. bdrm.   =   _____

8. unfurn. =   _____

9. drps.   =   _____

10. util.   =   _____

11. prkg.   =   _____

12. $ =   _____

A APT UNFURN FOR RENT
$1295 2 story. 3 bdrm, 2-1/2 bath,
Washer/dryer. Newly remodeled.
Garage. Pool. Tennis.   555-5634

B APT FURN FOR RENT
$590 lrg. 1 bdrm. All util.
Stove, refrigerator.
Security bldg.   555-5634

C APT UNFURN FOR RENT
$672 upper, quiet. Small bldg.
2 + 2. lrg. kitchen. Prkg.
New crpt., drps.   555-1002

B. Read about the apartments. Write the letters of the ads.

1. _B_ It has one big bedroom. You don't need a new stove or a refrigerator.
You don't pay for electricity or gas. It is safe.

2. ____ It has two floors. There are three bedrooms and 2 1/2 bathrooms.
You can swim there and play tennis.

3. ____ It is on the second floor in a small building. There are two bedrooms
and two bathrooms. There are new drapes and carpeting. There is room
for cars.

C. Write the words after the abbreviations.

| West | east | a week | location | transportation |
| North | near | a month | available | and |

1. loc. = _____

2. nr. = _____

3. e. = _____

4. & = _____

5. /mo. = _____

6. trans. = _____

7. W. = _____

8. N. = _____

9. avail. = _____

10. /wk. = _____

[A] **HOUSE FOR RENT**
$1900 Luxury. Oak Hills. 2-story.
Lrg. back yard. Pool. Garage.
Good loc. Nice neighborhood.
Children OK, no pets.   555-6000

[B] **HOUSE FOR SALE**
$180,000 3 + 2.
Crpt., drps. Gas. Private
prkg. 450 W. Spring St.,
Westdale   Call 555-6767

[C] **SINGLE APARTMENT**
$450/mo. Util. paid. Newly furn. bldg.
Laundry room. Nr. trans. 2 miles W.
of downtown, Security. Avail. 12/1.
Leave message for Pete   555-9090.

[D] **ROOM FOR RENT**
$25.50/wk. In 3-bdrm furn.
apt. Quiet. Private bath &
kitchen use. Nr. shopping.
1213 N. 4th St.

D. Read about the places. Write the letters of the ads.

1. ____ It's for one person. There's new furniture. You can wash your clothes in the building. You can walk to the bus stop. You can move there on December 1.

2. ____ It's not for rent. But you can buy it. There are three bedrooms and two bathrooms. It has carpeting and drapes. There's gas heat. There's room for cars.

3. ____ It's not an apartment or a house. It's a bedroom with a bathroom. You can cook in the kitchen. It's near stores. It isn't noisy.

4. ____ It's big. It's in a nice place. Children can live there. They can swim and play outside. But they can't have animals. There's a place for cars.

**E. Look at housing ads in the local newspaper. Write the abbreviations on the chalkboard and tell the words. Talk about the information.

BIG SALE
ONE TIME ONLY

PRICES GOOD THROUGH JANUARY 22

NO PAYMENTS BEFORE MARCH

LAST FOUR DAYS
LOW, LOW PRICES

LIVING ROOM FURNITURE

couches	*regular*	*$750*	**now**	**$665**
chairs	*regular*	*$298*	**now**	**$195**

Good Buys
on carpets and drapes

We rent furniture, too:
low monthly rates

May Furniture Company
12007 Spring Blvd.
Springdale

HOURS

Weekdays   10:00 a.m. - 5:30 p.m.
Sat.   12 noon - 5:00 p.m.

FREE PARKING

FREE DELIVERY

F.   Are these sentences about the ad true? Write *yes* or *no*.

1. yes   There's a furniture store on Spring Boulevard in the city of Springdale.

2. _____ This ad is from the newspaper on Friday, August 13.

3. _____ You can buy furniture now, and you can pay for it later.

4. _____ You can buy refrigerators, stoves, and washing machines on sale in this store.

5. _____ There's a sale on furniture for the living room.

6. _____ A couch usually costs $665. Now it costs $750.

7. _____ There are no carpets, drapes, or curtains in the store.

8. _____ The store is open seven days a week.

9. _____ You can buy or rent furniture from the store.

10. _____ You pay for parking and delivery of furniture to your house.

**G.   Look at newspaper sale ads for furniture and things for the house. In English class, talk about the ads. Answer these questions: Do you think the prices are very low? Do you buy things on sale? Do you save money?

PART TWO / INFORMATION

- Cities, States, Provinces, and Zip Codes ● Numbers and Amounts of Money
- Housing Applications

Abbreviations for States and Provinces

The postal service prefers these abbreviations for states and provinces in North America.

The United States											Canada	
AL	CO	GA	IN	MD	MS	NH	OH	SC	VA	WY	AB	NS
AK	CT	HI	KS	ME	MT	NJ	OK	SD	VT		BC	ON
AR	DC	IA	KY	MI	NC	NM	OR	TN	WA		MB	PQ
AZ	DE	ID	LA	MN	ND	NV	PA	TX	WI		NB	SK
CA	FL	IL	MA	MO	NE	NY	RI	UT	WV		NF	

A. What abbreviations do you use? Write them on the map.

Cities, States, and Zip Codes

San Francisco CA 94103

capital letter   zip code

B. Write the cities, states, and zip codes for

1. your home _____   3. your school _____

2. your job _____

Numbers and Amounts of Money	
100	one hundred
212	two hundred twelve
316	three hundred sixteen
660	six hundred sixty
998	nine hundred ninety-eight
1000	one thousand
4500	four thousand five hundred = forty-five hundred
5025	five thousand twenty-five
10,000	ten thousand
18,880	eighteen thousand eight hundred eighty
$5.31	five dollars and thirty-one cents = five thirty-one
$6.50/hr.	six dollars and fifty cents per hour = six fifty an hour
$77/wk.	seventy-seven dollars a week
$400/mo.	four hundred (dollars) a month
$22,000/yr.	twenty-two thousand (dollars) a year

C. Write the numbers and amounts of money.

1. one hundred thirty __130__

2. five hundred _____

3. seven hundred
   seventy-seven _____

4. two thousand
   four hundred ten _____

5. twelve thousand
   forty _____

6. thirty thousand
   two hundred six _____

7. ninety-eight dollars __$98__

8. fifteen sixty-three _____

9. seven eighty-nine
   an hour _____

10. three hundred
    sixty-two
    dollars a week _____

11. five hundred ten
    dollars a month _____

12. thirteen thousand
    nine hundred a year _____

13. the number of students in your class _____ the number of

    students with jobs _____ with houses _____

    with apartments _____

14. the amount of your rent every month _____ your electricity

    bill _____ your telephone bill _____

A Housing Application

APPLICATION TO RENT

NAME Walker   William Lee   HOME PHONE (313) 555-1068
     last,   first

DATE OF BIRTH 4 – 30 – 49
            month   day   year

	STREET ADDRESS	CITY, STATE	ZIP CODE	MANAGER	FROM	TO
NOW	720 Texas Pl. Apt. 111	Detroit MI	48220	Mr. Luis Gomez	1/86	Now

REASON FOR MOVING The apartment is too small for us.

	STREET ADDRESS	CITY, STATE	ZIP CODE	MANAGER	FROM	TO
BEFORE	2318 26th St. #16	Toledo Ohio	43604	Ms. Susan Chen	5/80	1/86

REASON FOR MOVING a new job in a new city

	NOW	BEFORE
JOB	teach school	work in a store
EMPLOYER	Evans Adult School	Books, Books, Books (Bookstore)
BUSINESS ADDRESS	717 N. Grant Ave. Detroit, Michigan	3064 1/2 Central Blvd. Toledo, Ohio
BUSINESS PHONE	(313) 555-8212	(419) 555-9781
PAY	$2,000/mo.	$320/wk.

PEOPLE IN APARTMENT	RELATIONSHIP	AGE	JOB
Emiko	wife	38	secretary
Peter	son	19	student
Amy	daughter	15	student

6/29/88   William L. Walker
date   signature of applicant

D. Write the information from the application on page 37.

William Lee Walker wants to rent an apartment. He is
1. the name

_____ years old. The manager of the new apartment can call him
2. a number

at _____ . Now William has an apartment
3. the phone number

at _____ ,
4. the address

_____ , _____ _____ .
5. the city   6. the state   7. the zip code

But it's too _____ for his family. He has a
8. reason for moving

_____ and two _____ . His _____ is nineteen
9. a relative   10. relatives   11. relative

years old. His daughter is _____ years old. Now William has a job at
12. a number

_____ . It's in _____ ,
13. the place   14. the city

_____ . His job before was in _____ , _____ .
15. the state   16. the city   17. the state

His pay now is _____ a month. His pay at his last job was
18. an amount

_____ a week. The date of the application is _____ .
19. an amount   20. the date

_____ **E.** **Print information about you in the application. Write your signature.**

APPLICATION TO RENT

NAME _____ HOME PHONE _____

　　　　　　　　last,　　　　　　first

　　　　　　DATE OF BIRTH _____

　　　　　　　　　　　month　　　day　　　year

	STREET ADDRESS	CITY, STATE	ZIP CODE	MANAGER	FROM	TO
NOW						

REASON FOR MOVING

BEFORE						

REASON FOR MOVING

	NOW	BEFORE
JOB		
EMPLOYER		
BUSINESS ADDRESS		
BUSINESS PHONE		
PAY		

PEOPLE IN APARTMENT	RELATIONSHIP	AGE	JOB

_____ _____

　　date　　　　　　　　　　signature of applicant

_____ ****F.** **Bring housing applications to class. Talk about the words and information. Answer these questions: How are they like the above application? How are they different?**

PART THREE / SPELLING

- The Vowels *ai, ay, ee, ea, ie, oa, oo*
- Contrast with the Spellings *a* (-e), *e* (-e), *i* (-e), *o* (-e), *u* (-e)

Letters	a-e	e-e	i-e	o-e	u-e
Examples	state	Pete	price	code	rule
Letters	ai ay	ee ea	ie	oa	oo
Examples	wait pay	feet heat	die	road	cool

Use *ay* and *ie* at the end of words or word parts.

A. **Listen to the sentences. Write the vowel letters.**

ai	ay	ee	ea	ie	oa	oo

1. w a i t   2. p___   3. tr___   4. ___t

5. t___   6. b___t   7. f___d

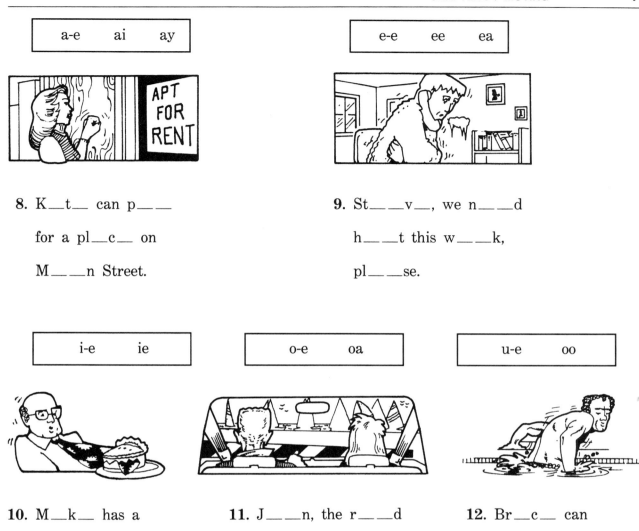

a-e   ai   ay

8. K__t__ can p____

for a pl__c__ on

M____n Street.

e-e   ee   ea

9. St____v__, we n____d

h____t this w____k,

pl____se.

i-e   ie

10. M__k__ has a

n__c__ t____ in

his p____ .

o-e   oa

11. J____n, the r____d

to the b____ts

is cl__s__d.

u-e   oo

12. Br__c__ can

__s__ the p____l

at sc____l.

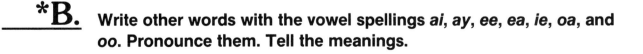

*B. **Write other words with the vowel spellings *ai*, *ay*, *ee*, *ea*, *ie*, *oa*, and *oo*. Pronounce them. Tell the meanings.**

Letters	a	e	i	o	u
Examples	m<u>a</u>n	m<u>e</u>n	h<u>i</u>m	r<u>o</u>d	b<u>u</u>t

____ C. Listen to the words. Write the vowel letters.

a	e	i	o	u	ai	ea	i-e	oa	oo

1. m__n on

   M____n Street

2. What do the

   m__n m____n?

3. T__m has

   the t__m__.

4. a r__d on

   the r____d

5. B__t I

   want b____ts.

____ D. Now read the words and sentences from A and C aloud.

PART FOUR / READ AND WRITE

● Short Letters

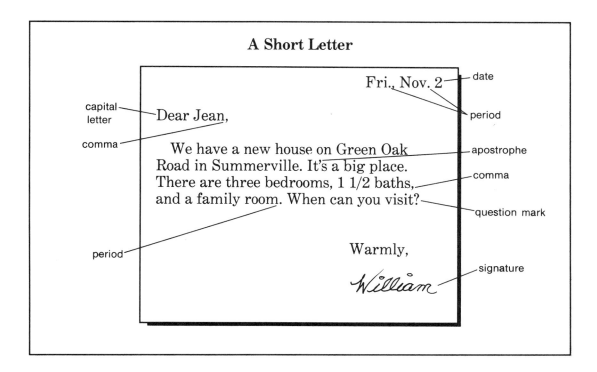

A Short Letter

A. Change the small letters to capital letters. Write the periods, question marks, commas, and apostrophes.

wed   nov   7

dear   kate

thank   you   for   your   letter   can   i   visit   you   on   the   weekend   do   you

need   any   furniture   for   your   new   place   there   s   a   couch   in   my   garage

it   s   green   i   have   a   table   some   chairs   and   some   dishes,   too

Love,

Bruce

_____ **B.** **Cover the words under each line with paper. Listen and write. Then check your writing.**

Dec. 14, 19XX

_____

Dear Pete,

_____   _____

We live on White Oak Road now.   It's a nice place.

_____   _____

It's furnished.   There's yellow carpeting in the living room.

_____

It has a red couch, a table, chairs, and a dishwasher.

_____   _____

When can you see it?   Write us soon.

Love,
Kate

_____ **C.** **Look at the ads. Finish the letters about the places.**

APT FOR RENT
$895
2 bdrm, beautifully
furn. blue crpt.,
drps. Nr. schools
& trans. Util. pd.

Dear _____ ,
    1.

    This letter is from my new <u>apartment</u> . There are two
                   2.

_____ . It's beautifully _____ . It has blue _____
3.   **4.**   **5.**

and _____ . It's _____ schools and _____ .
   6.   **7.**   **8.**

It's expensive, but I don't pay for _____ . Can you visit me?
                                   9.

    Warmly,

    _____
    10.   your signature

HOUSE FOR SALE
$96,000
1-bdrm. 1 1/2 baths.
Garage, laundry room.
Good loc. 3 miles n. of
downtown.

Dear _____ ,
      11.

    When can you see our new _____ ? It has
                                  12.

only one _____ , but there are _____ bathrooms,
          13.   **14.**

a _____ , and a _____ room. It's in a good
 15.   **16.**

_____ only three miles _____ of downtown!
17.   **18.**

      Love,

      _____

      19. your signature

_____ ***D.** **Write a letter about your room, apartment, or house.**

Food and Things

COMPETENCIES: Understanding restaurant menus, bills, tax, and tips

Solving math problems

Understanding measurements and labels

Writing shopping lists

SPELLING: The consonants *s*, *c*, *k*, *sh*, *ch*

Plural and possessive words

GRAMMAR FOCUS: The verb *be*

PART ONE / READ AND UNDERSTAND

● Restaurant Menus

A. Check the foods from the menu on page 48.

1. ✓ a bowl of soup

2. _____ a Mexican breakfast

3. _____ different kinds of hamburgers

4. _____ a chili and vegetable sandwich

5. _____ a special dinner every day of the week

6. _____ chicken or turkey salad

7. _____ fish with soup or salad, potatoes, and vegetables

8. _____ a cheese pizza

9. _____ coffee, tea, or milk

10. _____ a choice of desserts

11. _____ hot strawberry cheese pie

12. _____ apple pie with ice cream

B. Write the prices of these foods from the menu.

1. the Bacon Cheeseburger $2.25

2. a steak sandwich _____

3. soup with fruit salad _____

4. a spaghetti dinner _____

5. a large glass of milk _____

6. a piece of pie _____

C. For each number, one kind of food is more expensive. Circle the letter a or b.

1. (a.) a bowl of vegetable soup
   b. a cup of the soup of the day

2. a. a chicken and cheese sandwich
   b. a steak sandwich

3. a. a spaghetti dinner
   b. a roast beef dinner

4. a. a soup and salad
   b. a chef's salad

5. a. a cup of coffee
   b. a soft drink

6. a. a piece of cheesecake
   b. a piece of apple pie

7. a. strawberry pie
   b. pie à la mode

8. a. a daily dinner special
   b. dessert

MENU

Soups

Soup of the Day	Bowl .... .95	Cup .... .75
Vegetable Soup	Bowl .... .95	Cup .... .75

Hamburger Specialties

The Basic Burger 1.95
(with Lettuce, Tomato, and
Dressing on a Bun)

The Bacon Cheeseburger 2.25
(with Bacon and Cheese on
a Bun or Toast)

The Chiliburger Special 2.85
(with Cheese and Chili Beans on a Bun)

More Sandwiches

(on Your Choice of Bun, Toast, or Bread, with French Fries)

Chicken and Cheese 2.50	Steak 3.00
Bacon, Lettuce, and Tomato 2.35	Fish 2.65

SOUP AND SALAD 2.00
(a Cup of the Soup of the
Day with Your Choice of
Vegetable or Fruit Salad)

SOUP AND SANDWICH 2.00
(a Cup of the Soup of the
Day with Your Choice of
1/2 Sandwich)

Daily Dinner Specials

(available from 3 to 11 p.m. daily, noon to 11 p.m. Sunday)

****

(with Choice of Soup or Salad, Potatoes, and Vegetable)

MONDAY	Spaghetti 3.25	**FRIDAY**	Fish 4.15
TUESDAY	Chicken 3.95	**SATURDAY**	Steak 5.60
WEDNESDAY	Meat Loaf 3.55	**SUNDAY**	Roast Beef 5.25
THURSDAY	Turkey 4.00		

Salads

Chef's Salad 3.60	Fruit Salad 3.60

Beverages

Coffee .... .50	Hot or Iced Tea .... .50	Hot Chocolate ...... .50
Milk .... Regular .... .50	Large .... .75	Soft Drinks .... .55

Desserts

Dish of Ice Cream: Vanilla, Chocolate, Strawberry .... .80

Cheesecake 1.30	Chocolate Cake 1.40
Pie: Apple, Strawberry .... 1.10 .... à la Mode 1.60

D. On the menu, find the answers to these questions. Circle the letters *a*, *b*, *c*, or *d*. Some questions have more than one right answer.

1. Can you get a bowl of vegetable soup every day?
   - a. yes
   - b. no
   - c. only on weekdays
   - d. only for lunch

2. What does the Chiliburger Special have on it?
   - a. soup
   - b. cheese and beans
   - c. chili in a bowl
   - d. turkey

3. How many kinds of sandwiches are there (not hamburgers)?
   - a. two
   - b. four
   - c. seven
   - d. thirteen

4. What is Wednesday's dinner special?
   - a. bean soup
   - b. meat loaf
   - c. turkey with bread
   - d. spaghetti

5. What costs $3.60?
   - a. a fruit or chef's salad
   - b. a dinner
   - c. a sandwich
   - d. pie

6. Does the Basic Burger come on a bun, on toast, or on bread?
   - a. on a bun
   - b. on toast
   - c. on bread
   - d. all of these

7. What foods are beverages?
   - a. beans
   - b. coffee
   - c. iced tea
   - d. milk

8. What foods are desserts?
   - a. vegetables
   - b. strawberry ice cream
   - c. pizza pie
   - d. cake

*E. Work together. Look at the menu on page 48. Ask and answer questions about prices and kinds of food.

**F. Look at menus in restaurants. Write some new words. In English class, talk about the words. (Maybe the restaurant can give you a menu. Then you can bring it to class and talk about it.)

PART TWO / INFORMATION

● Restaurant Bills ● Mathematics ● Tax and Tips

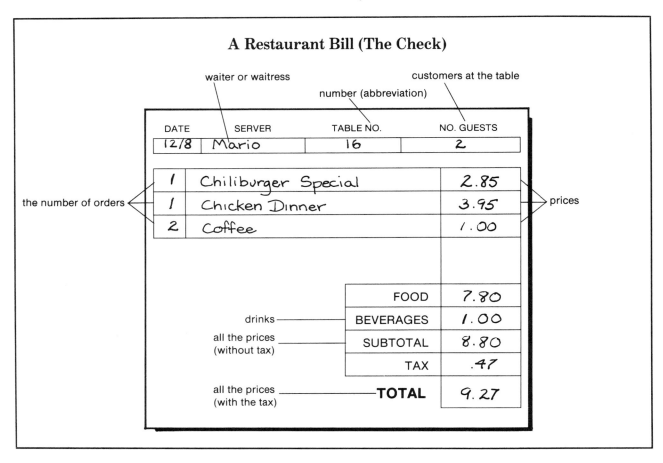

A Restaurant Bill (The Check)

_____**A.** **Find the information and answer the questions about the bill.**

1. What is the date? _December 8_   Who is the waiter? _____

2. How many guests are there? _____ Is this a bill for breakfast? _____

3. What is one customer's food order? _____

4. What is the second customer's order? _____

5. How many cups of coffee do they have? _____

6. How much is one cup of coffee? _____

7. How much is the tax on the food and beverages? _____

8. Is the bill correct? (Look at the menu on page 48.) _____

9. How much do the customers pay in total? _____

Mathematics (Math)

Addition	Subtraction	Multiplication	Division
$1.50	$5.80	$2.20	3.25
+ .75	−1.40	× 3	2 ⟌ 6.50
total $2.25	$4.40	$6.60	

$$4 + 3 + 7 \overset{\text{equals}}{=} 14 \qquad 18 - 7 \overset{\text{equals}}{=} 11 \qquad 1.25 \times 4 \overset{\text{equals}}{=} 5.00 \qquad 12 \div 4 \overset{\text{equals}}{=} 3$$

plus   minus   times   divided by

B. **Read. Then write these symbols.**

+	−	×	=

Is this bill correct? I'm not sure. Let me check it.

1. Let's see now ... a bowl of soup, a chiliburger, and a cup of tea for me. That's $4.30.

2. Two fish sandwiches for you.

3. Pie à la mode and cheesecake for dessert.

4. No, that's not right. Not pie à la mode. Just pie.

5. So ... your dinner and mine and our desserts together.

.95 + 2.85 + .50 = 4.30

2.65   2   5.30

1.60   1.30   2.90

2.90   .50   2.40

4.30   5.30   2.40   12.00

Tax and Tips

In a restaurant, customers pay sales tax on the food. The tax is a percentage (%) of the total bill. Also, they usually leave a tip for the waiter or waitress. This tip is also a percentage of the total. It is usually 10 to 20 percent.

Percentage

6% of \$1 = 1 × .06 = .06
percent   (point oh six)

10% of \$2.50 = 2.50 × .10 = .25

C. **Read. Then write these symbols.**

÷	+	×	=

1. The total bill is \$12.00.
   Tax in this state is 6%.

2. What's the total?

3. How about a tip?
   We can leave 15%.

4. With a \$2 tip, that's \$14.72.
   We can share the bill equally.

5. So it's \$7.36 each. O.K.?

12.00 × .06 = .72

12.00   .72   12.72

12.72   .15   1.91

12.72   2.00   14.72

14.72   2   7.36

D. Look at the menu on page 48. Write the prices and total the bills.

DATE	SERVER	TABLE NO.		NO. GUESTS	
8/21	Joan	11		3	

1	Vegetable Soup (Cup)	.75
1	Basic Burger	
2	Steak Sandwich	
2	Tea	
1	Milk (Large)	
	FOOD AND BEVERAGES SUBTOTAL	
	6% TAX	
	TOTAL	

DATE	SERVER	TABLE NO.		NO. GUESTS	
10/2	Steve	4		2	

1	Meat Loaf Dinner	
1	Chef's Salad	
2	Soft Drinks	
1	Ice Cream	
2	Cheesecake	
	FOOD AND BEVERAGES SUBTOTAL	
	5% TAX	
	TOTAL	

*E. Read. Write the math. Then write the answers to the questions.

A family has dinner at a restaurant. The father has a chicken and cheese sandwich for $2.50. The mother has a bacon cheeseburger for $2.25. The son has a spaghetti dinner for $3.25. The family has two cups of tea for 50¢ each and a soft drink for 55¢. They share two desserts: a piece of chocolate cake for $1.40 and a piece of pie à la mode for $1.60.

1. How much are the food and beverages? _____

2. The tax in this state is 5%. How much is the tax? _____

3. The mother and father want to leave a 10% tip. How much do they

   leave? _____

4. How much do they spend on dinner in total? _____

**F. Check the prices and the math on your next restaurant bill.

PART THREE / SPELLING

● The Consonants *s, c, k, sh, ch* ● Plural and Possessive Words

Spelling	Examples	
For the "s" sound, use the letter *c* only before *e, i,* or *y*. Use *s* before all other letters.	<u>c</u>elery <u>s</u>oup	re<u>c</u>eive <u>s</u>alad
For the "k" sound, use the letter *k* before *e, i,* or *y* or at the end of syllables. Use *c* before all other letters.	tur<u>k</u>ey <u>c</u>up	stea<u>k</u> <u>c</u>oo<u>k</u>ies
Use the letters *sh* for one sound.	<u>sh</u>ake	di<u>sh</u>es
Use the letters *ch* for one sound.	<u>ch</u>erries	sandwi<u>ch</u>

A. Listen to the words. Write the consonant letters. | s   c   k   sh   ch |

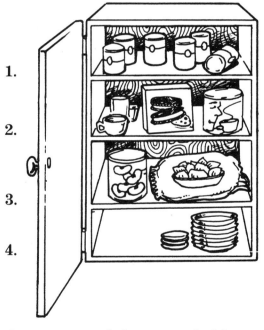

1.

2.

3.

4.

1. <u>s</u>oup, __alad, a __andwich, __elery

2. __ups, a __an of __offee, __oo__ies, __a__e, ba__on, tur__ey

3. ____ili, potato ____ips, ____eese, ____erries, ____ocolate

4. di____es, fi____, a milk____ake

_____ ***B.** **Write other words with the letters *s*, *c*, *k*, *sh*, and *ch* at the beginning of syllables. Tell the meanings.**

Singular	Spelling	Plural
glass sandwich tomato	1. For the plural form, add *-es* to *-s, -z, -sh, -ch, -x,* and *-o* (*-o* after a consonant).	glass**es** sandwich**es** tomato**es**
baby fry	2. These words end in *-y* after a consonant. Change the *y* to *i* and add *-es*.	bab**ies** fr**ies**
shelf knife	3. These words end in *-f* or *-fe*. Change the *f* to *v* and add *-s* or *-es*.	shel**ves** kni**ves**
steak hamburger	4. Add *-s* to other words.	steak**s** hamburger**s**

Here are some words with irregular plural forms.

Singular	person	man	woman	child	foot	tooth	fish
Plural	people	men	women	children	feet	teeth	fish

_____ **C.** **Write the plural words on the lines.**

A Shopping List

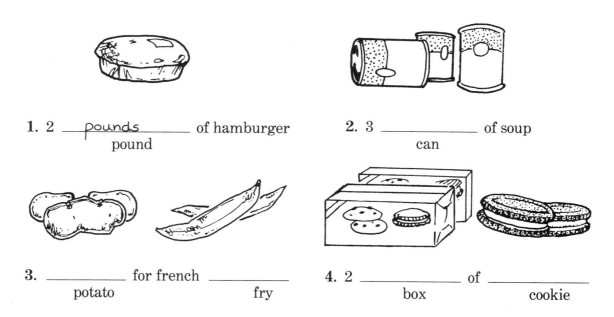

1. 2 <u>pounds</u> of hamburger
       pound

2. 3 _____ of soup
       can

3. _____ for french _____
     potato   fry

4. 2 _____ of _____
       box   cookie

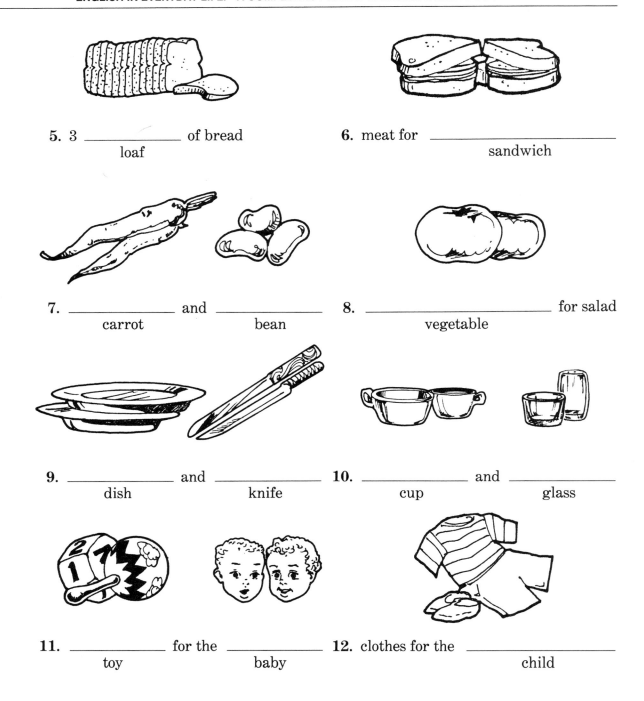

5. 3 _____ of bread
   loaf

6. meat for _____
                  sandwich

7. _____ and _____
   carrot   bean

8. _____ for salad
     vegetable

9. _____ and _____
   dish   knife

10. _____ and _____
    cup   glass

11. _____ for the _____
    toy   baby

12. clothes for the _____
                     child

____ **D.** **Now read the shopping list aloud.**

____ ***E.** **Write the plural forms of other words. Tell the singular forms and the meanings.**

	Spelling	Possessive
David my brother the children	1. These singular and plural words don't end in -s. Add -'s for the possessive form.	David's my brother's the children's
my parents the waitresses	2. These plural words end in -s. Add only an apostrophe (') for the possessive form.	my parents' the waitresses'

F. Write the possessive words on the lines.

My ___parents'___ favorite restaurant is _____
   1. parents   2. Sam

Sandwich Shop. My _____ favorite food there is a steakburger.
                  3. brother

My _____ favorites are on the _____
   4. sisters   5. children

menu. I like the _____ and _____ fast and friendly
                 6. waiters   7. waitresses

service. The _____ prices are low. The _____
            8. restaurant   9. family

bill is never over $25.

PART FOUR / READ AND WRITE

● Measurements ● Labels ● Shopping Lists

Measurements

wt. = weight	fl. = fluid	l. = liter(s)
lb. = pound(s)	gal. = gallon(s)	
oz. = ounce(s)	qt. = quart(s)	3.78 = three point
g. = gram(s)	pt. = pint(s)	seven eight

A. Find the answers to these questions on page 59. Write them on the lines.

1. What foods are in cans? _____beans_____ In cartons? _____

_____ _____ In loaves? _____

In jars? _____ In packages? _____

2. How many cups are there in a pint? _____ In a quart? _____

Quarts in a gallon? _____ Fluid ounces in a half gallon? _____

Liters in a quart? _____

3. How many ounces are there in a pound? _____ Things in a

dozen? _____

4. How much is one ounce of Mrs. Brown's Baked Beans in a small

can? ($.80 ÷ 16 = ?) _____ One ounce of Mrs. Brown's Baked

Beans in a large can? ($1.16 ÷ 29 = ?) _____ One ounce of the

store brand of beans? ($.87 ÷ 29 = ?) _____ Which can is the

best buy? _____

5. How much is one ounce of nonfat milk in a half-gallon carton? _____

One ounce of cream in a pint carton? _____ One ounce of whole

wheat bread? _____ Of the store brand of white bread? _____

1 gal. = 2 half gal. = 4 qts. = 8 pts. = 16 cups   1 doz = 12

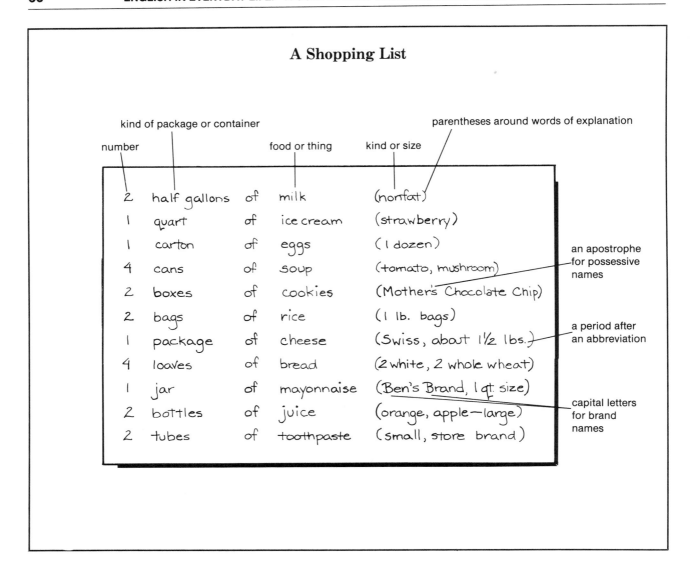

A Shopping List

number	kind of package or container		food or thing	kind or size	
2	half gallons	of	milk	(nonfat)	
1	quart	of	ice cream	(strawberry)	
1	carton	of	eggs	(1 dozen)	
4	cans	of	soup	(tomato, mushroom)	
2	boxes	of	cookies	(Mother's Chocolate Chip)	
2	bags	of	rice	(1 lb. bags)	
1	package	of	cheese	(Swiss, about 1½ lbs.)	
4	loaves	of	bread	(2 white, 2 whole wheat)	
1	jar	of	mayonnaise	(Ben's Brand, 1 qt. size)	
2	bottles	of	juice	(orange, apple—large)	
2	tubes	of	toothpaste	(small, store brand)	

parentheses around words of explanation

an apostrophe for possessive names

a period after an abbreviation

capital letters for brand names

B. Change the small letters to capital letters. Write the periods, apostrophes, and parentheses.

2 half gal of whole milk not nonfat

1 lb package of cheese from dee s dairy

2 doz eggs The brand is fresh farms.

vegetables for a chef s salad lettuce, tomatoes, and celery

1 bag of potato chips lori skidder s brand, 12 oz size

C. Cover the words under each line with paper. Listen and write the list. Check your writing.

1. _____

   3 small cans of cream of chicken soup (the store brand)

2. _____

   lettuce, celery, tomatoes, and carrots for salad

3. _____

   some 3.5 oz. packages of lunch meat (turkey, beef)

4. _____

   a 4 oz. jar of coffee (The brand is Top Choice.)

5. _____

   a bag of Mrs. Chip's sugar cookies

D. Choose things from page 60 and write a shopping list.

_____

_____

_____

_____

_____

_____

_____

_____

**E. Write your own shopping list. Exchange lists and check them. Then go to the market together and buy the things on the list. Cook, eat, and have a good time.

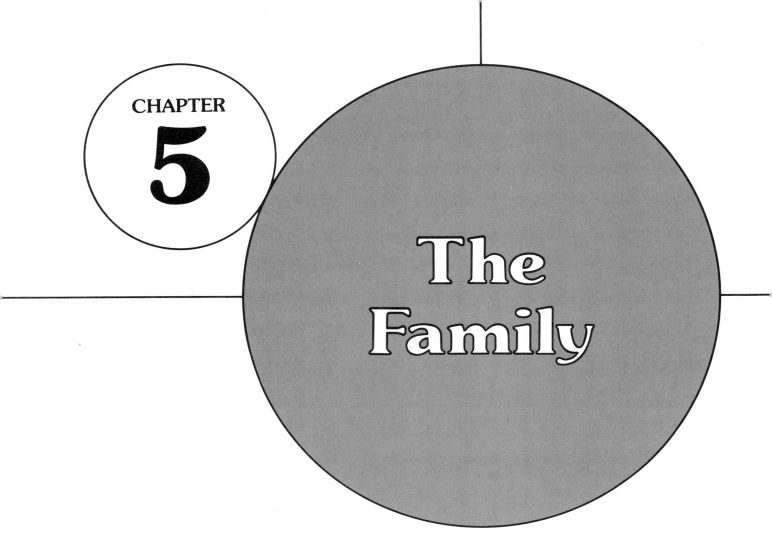

CHAPTER 5

The Family

COMPETENCIES: Knowing about kinds of families
Understanding ads and announcements about families
Understanding area codes, time zones, kinds of telephone calls, and telephone bills
Taking telephone messages

SPELLING: The consonants *l, r, d, t, th*
The -(*e*)*s* ending

GRAMMAR FOCUS: The present tense (-*s* form on verbs)
Infinitives after common verbs
Frequency words

PART ONE / READ AND UNDERSTAND

● Kinds of Families ● Ads and Announcements about Families

Kinds of Families

What does the word *family* mean in the United States and Canada? In North American culture, people usually live in small groups. Many children live with both their mother and father, but some children live with only one parent. Their grandparents, aunts, uncles, and cousins are their *relatives*. Relatives can visit a family, of course, but they don't usually live with the family. Some unmarried couples live together, and many people live alone.

The members of some families are very close. In other families, the members do not spend a lot of time together. Some families try to get help with their problems from counselors. In the United States and Canada, many marriages end in divorce. Then the parents have to make agreements about child care and support.

In other cultures, people stay together in big family groups. Sometimes husbands and wives, their children, their parents or in-laws, and their sisters and brothers live in the same house. In these cultures, the word *family* has a different meaning.

A. Are these sentences true? Answer *yes* or *no*.

1. _no_ People in the United States and Canada usually live together in big families.

2. _____ In the United States and Canada, children sometimes live with only one parent.

3. _____ People don't always live in family groups. Some unmarried couples live together, and some people live alone.

4. _____ All the members of close families spend a lot of time at group counseling centers.

5. _____ In divorce, parents have to make agreements about child care and support.

6. _____ In other cultures, people sometimes live with their relatives. Husbands and wives, parents and in-laws, children, brothers, and sisters can live together.

*B. Answer these questions.

1. In your culture, what kinds of family groups do people live in (with many relatives, only parents and children, unmarried couples, etc.)?

2. Do you like big families? Why or why not?

A

PINOCCHIO'S PIZZA PALACE

Food and Fun for the Family
Italian Sausage • Meatball and Spaghetti
Video Games • Music
Cartoon Films on the Weekend!
Open 11 a.m. to 10 p.m.
230 Pepperoni Place

B

FAMILY FILMS

Movie Fun for Everyone!
Hey, it's Bogi Bear!
The Story of Supercat!
Sat. & Sun. Apr. 1-2

The Kiddycat Theater   **3000 Kartoon**

C

THE HELP CENTER
Marriage and Family Counseling
Couples   Families   Children
We Accept All Kinds of Insurance;
Day, Night, and Saturday Appointments
208-4242   110 Grandview Dr., Grandview

D

ENGAGED Mr. Orem Mizrahi announces the engagement of his daughter, Salma Mizrahi, to Robert Goldstein, son of Mr. and Mrs. Sam Goldstein, Kingstown. Miss Mizrahi is a counselor at the Grandview Help Center. Her fiance manages Pinnochio's Pizza Palace. The couple plans to marry June 21.

E

FAMILY PLANNING CENTER
Birth Control or Counseling
Pregnancy Testing   Blood Tests   Low Cost
Women's and Children's Health Care
Information for a Happy and Healthy Family

F

BIRTH Roland Gonzalez and Lucy Nkrumah-Gonzalez announce the birth of their daughter, Rosa May. The grandparents are Mr. and Mrs. Silvio Gonzalez of La Paz, Bolivia, and Mr. Ja-Ja Nkrumah, of Ibadan, Nigeria.

C. On the lines, write the letters of the above announcements and ads.

1. _F_ It announces the birth of a baby to a couple from two countries.

2. ____ You can get information about family planning and birth control at this center.

3. ____ This ad tells about movies especially for children.

4. ____ This announcement tells about the engagement and future marriage of a man and a woman.

5. ____ This service gives information and help to families with problems.

6. ____ This is a good family restaurant. It has games and shows movies, and children like the food.

**D. Look at family entertainment ads and announcements in the local newspaper. Talk about the words and the information.

PART TWO /INFORMATION

● Area Codes and Time Zones ● Kinds of Telephone Calls ● Telephone Bills

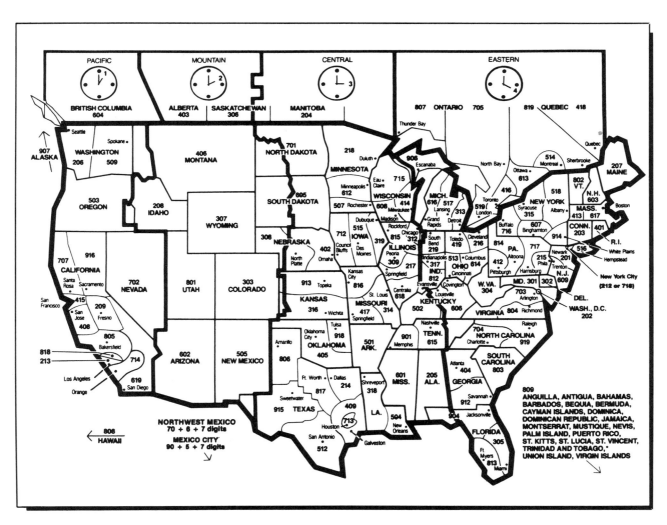

A. Find the information on page 65. Write it on the lines.

1. How can you call these places without help from an operator?

   Vancouver, British Columbia, Canada: You dial ___1___ + ___604___ + the local number.

   Portland, Oregon: You dial _____+ _____ + the local number.

   Little Rock, Arkansas: You dial _____ + _____ + the local number.

   Reno, Nevada: You dial _____ + _____ + the local number.

   Mexico City, Mexico: You dial _____ + _____ + the local number.

   Think of a relative or friend of yours in North America. How can you call him or her directly? You dial _____ + _____ + _____ .

2. You want to make a call from San Diego, California, at 1:00. What's the time in Denver, Colorado? _____ In Austin, Texas? _____ In Toledo, Ohio? _____

3. You want to make a call from Las Vegas, Nevada, at 3:30 in the afternoon. What's the time in Albuquerque, New Mexico? _____ In Madison, Wisconsin? _____ In New York City? _____

4. You want to make a call from Miami, Florida, at midnight. What's the time in Chicago, Illinois? _____ In Phoenix, Arizona? _____ In Los Angeles, California? _____

For discounts of the full weekday rates, call evenings, nights, & weekends.

	M	T	W	T	F	S	S	Dial-direct		
8 A.M. to 5 P.M.								Full (weekday) rates	Lower (evening) rates 30% discount	Lowest (night & weekend) rates 60% discount
5 P.M. to 11 P.M.										
11 P.M. to 8 A.M.										

_____ **B.** You want to make a long-distance call. Look at the time-rate schedule on page 66. For each group, write $ before the least expensive time(s), $$ before the time(s) for a 30% discount and $$$ before the most expensive times(s).

Tuesday	Wednesday	Saturday
$$$ 9:00 a.m.	_____ 7:30 a.m.	_____ 9:15 a.m.
_____ 3:00 p.m.	_____ 11:30 a.m.	_____ 12:00 p.m. (noon)
_____ 10:00 p.m.	_____ 5:30 p.m.	_____ 6:45 p.m.
_____ 12:00 a.m. (midnight)	_____ 10:30 p.m.	_____ 11:30 p.m.

Station-to-Station, Person-to-Person, Collect, and International Calls

For a station-to-station call, you pay for the call if anyone answers the phone. For a person-to-person call, you pay only if you speak to a specific person. In a collect call, the other person pays. For all kinds of calls except station-to-station, you need the operator's help. Dial 0 + the area code + the local number. These kinds of calls are more expensive.

You can call other countries directly, too. For a station-to-station call, dial

1. 011 (the international code)
2. the country code
3. the city routing code
4. the local telephone number

Dial "0" for operator if the country and city code are not in your telephone book. For other kinds of calls (person-to-person, collect, etc.), dial 01 instead of 011.

Here are some examples of country and city codes.

Argentina	54	**Greece**	30	**Monaco**	33
Buenos Aires	1	Athens	1	All points	93
Cordoba	51	Piraeus	1		
				Nigeria	234
Austria	43	**Japan**	81	Ibadan	22
Graz	316	Kyoto	75		
Linz	732	Osaka	6	**Saudi Arabia**	966
Vienna	222	Toyko	3	Riyadh	1

____ C. Find the information on page 67. Write it on the lines.

1. For what kinds of calls do you need the operator's help?

   person-to-person, collect

2. For what countries and cities are these telephone numbers?

   011 + 43 + 222 + 42 71 86: _____ , _____

   011 + 81 + 75 + 78 11 23: _____ , _____

   011 + 234 + 22 + 67 77 77: _____ , _____

3. What do you dial for these places?

   Cordoba, Argentina (station-to-station): ____ + ____ + ____ + the local number

   Athens, Greece (station-to-station): ____ + ____ + ____ + the local number

   any place in Monaco (person-to-person): ____ + ____ + ____ + the local number

   Riyadh, Saudi Arabia (collect): ____ + ____ + ____ + the local number

____ **D. In your local telephone book, find the country and city codes for some of your relatives and friends outside the United States and Canada. (You can ask the operator, too.) Write them here.

Country	Country Code	City	City Code
Colombia	57	Bogotá	1

A Telephone Bill

NAME				NUMBER		DATE	
PAGE, MARGARET BROWN				555-2450		DEC. 01, 19XX	

		AMOUNT OF LAST BILL	63.54
	11/ 5 PAYMENT RECEIVED		63.54CR
	***BALANCE FROM LAST MONTH	$.00	
	OTHER CHARGES AND SERVICES	$10.75	
	***TOTAL MONTHLY SERVICE RATE 11/28 - 12/27		12.90

		LONG DISTANCE			MINUTE	TYPE	
810PM	10/ 8	LONG BEACH	CA	213 555-5726	1	DE	.18
414PM	10/ 8	DENVER	CO	303 555-8932	1	DN	.26
323PM	10/12	DETROIT	MI	303 555-5500	41	SCN	9.83
216PM	10/22	LOS ANGELES	CA	213 555-1845	6	DD	.93
1048AM	10/22	AKRON	OH	216 555-2937	122	SCD	5.77
1010AM	10/31	DURANGO	MX	521 555-2678	26	DN	8.91
1251PM	11/ 5	DURANGO	MX	521 555-2678	25	DD	21.90

TOTAL LONG DISTANCE CHARGES	47.78
FEDERAL TAX	2.37
CITY TAX	2.37
STATE TAX	.23
TOTAL DUE	51.75

MIN	=	NUMBER OF MINUTES	D	=	DAY
D	=	DIRECT DIALING	E	=	EVENING
S	=	STATION-TO-STATION	N	=	NIGHT
P	=	PERSON-TO-PERSON			
C	=	COLLECT			

E. Find the information in the telephone bill. Write it on the lines.

1. the telephone number of the receiver of this bill

   (the account number) _____

2. the date of the bill _____ the amount of last month's bill _____

   Did someone pay that bill?   (yes or no) _____

3. the cost of one month's service (without long-distance charges) _____

4. the number of long-distance calls to places in the United States _____ to places

   in other countries _____ the total cost of long-distance calls _____

5. the number of collect calls _____ of person-to-person calls _____ of directly

   dialed calls in the evening _____

6. the date of the call(s) to Denver, Colorado _____ to Durango, Mexico

   _____ _____

7. the amount of the total bill (with tax and other charges) _____

**F. Bring a telephone bill to class. Talk about it.

PART THREE / SPELLING

● The Consonants *l, r, d, t, th* ● The -(e)s Ending

Letters	l	r	d	t	th
Examples	local	relative	divorce	time	third
	alone	parents	Canada	entertain	these
	dial	father	code	night	other

 A. Listen to the words. Write the consonant letters. | l   r   d |

1. I __ike __arge

   fami__ies.

2. My siste__'s

   __efrige__ato__

   is in he__ __oom.

d

3. Can I __ial my

   __aughter __irectly?

t

4. What's the __o__al

   bill with __ax?

th

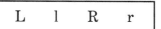

L   l   R   r

5. I __ink my

mo__er, fa__er,

and bro__er

are __ere.

6. Ou__ __e__atives

__ive in __ittle

__ock, Arkansas.

d   t

r   d   t

7. I __on't see my

__ad a lo__ of the

__ime. He lives in

Cana__a, and we live

in Flori__a.

8. Ou__ pa__ents

en__e__ __ain

__ela__ives in the

__ining __oom.

_____ **B.**   **Now read the sentences from A aloud.**

_____ ***C.**   **Write other words with the letters *l*, *r*, *d*, *t*, and *th*. Tell the meanings.**

	Spelling	-(e)s Form
miss does	**1.** Add -es to -s, -z, -sh, -ch, -x and -o (after a consonant).	miss**es** do**es**
fly study	**2.** These words end in -y after a consonant. Change the y to i. Add -es.	fl**ies** stud**ies**
stay buy	**3.** These words end in y after a vowel. Add -s.	stay**s** buy**s**
work	**4.** For other words, add -s.	work**s**
have	**5.** This form is irregular.	**has**

D. Add -(e)s to the words and write them on the lines.

My relatives live in Canada. My sister ___has___ a good job. She

                            1. have

_____ in a laboratory. Her husband _____ the children all

2. work   **3.** watch

day. At night he _____ to school. He _____ English, but

            4. go   **5.** teach

he _____ to change jobs. She _____ home at night and

   6. want   **7.** stay

_____ . She _____ to spend time with the children, too.

8. study   **9.** try

My brother _____ a hotel. He _____ interesting work,

     10. manage   **11.** do

and he _____ . He _____ a plane, too. He _____

    12. travel   **13.** fly   **14.** like

his job a lot.

E. Now read the above story aloud.

PART FOUR / READ AND WRITE

● Telephone Messages

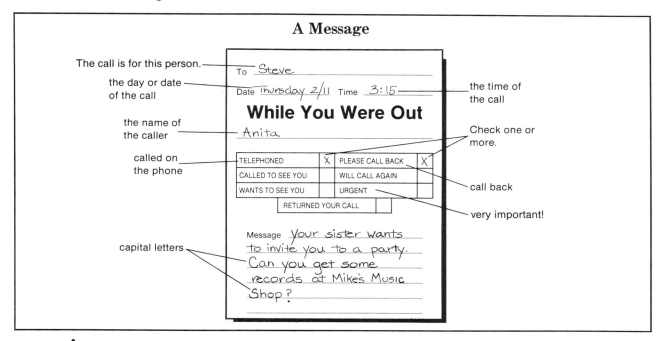

A Message

The call is for this person.
the day or date of the call
the name of the caller
called on the phone
capital letters

To Steve
Date Thursday 2/11 Time 3:15

While You Were Out

Anita

TELEPHONED	X	PLEASE CALL BACK	X	
CALLED TO SEE YOU		WILL CALL AGAIN		
WANTS TO SEE YOU		URGENT		
RETURNED YOUR CALL				

Message Your sister wants to invite you to a party. Can you get some records at Mike's Music Shop?

the time of the call
Check one or more.
call back
very important!

A. **Change the small letters to capital letters. Write the periods, question marks, commas, and apostrophes.**

MESSAGE can your mother use your car hers doesn t work it s at carl s carcare garage do you need it today she doesn t want to take your brother s car it s too big for her she has to go to a meeting at 7:00 please call her back

B. **Cover the words under each line with paper. Listen and write. Then check your writing.**

1. _____

Your children want to go to the movies this afternoon.

2. _____

Can they eat dinner at Pete's Pizza Place after that?

3. _____

Your daughter needs some money.

4. _____

She doesn't have any. She wants to buy cat food.

C. Read the conversations and write messages from them.

To <u>Mr. Thurman</u>

Date _____ Time _____

While You Were Out

_____

TELEPHONED		PLEASE CALL BACK	
CALLED TO SEE YOU		WILL CALL AGAIN	
WANTS TO SEE YOU		URGENT	
	RETURNED YOUR CALL		

Message _____

_____

_____

_____

_____

_____

1. Can I please speak to Mr. Thurman?

He's not available right now. Can I take a message?

Yes, please. This is the Westside Counseling Office. Please tell him we have to change his 4:30 appointment. Can he please call us before noon?

2. Is your father there, please? This is Linda Ruth Lane.

He can't come to the phone now. Do you want to leave a message?

Yes, I do. I'm the secretary at the Family Planning Center. We need some information from him. He can call me between 1:00 and 5:30.

To _____

Date _____ Time _____

While You Were Out

_____

TELEPHONED		PLEASE CALL BACK	
CALLED TO SEE YOU		WILL CALL AGAIN	
WANTS TO SEE YOU		URGENT	
	RETURNED YOUR CALL		

Message _____

_____

_____

_____

_____

3.

While You Were Out

To _____

Date _____ Time _____

TELEPHONED		PLEASE CALL BACK	
CALLED TO SEE YOU		WILL CALL AGAIN	
WANTS TO SEE YOU		URGENT	

RETURNED YOUR CALL

Message _____

_____

_____

_____

_____

_____

_____

**D. Work together. Play roles in phone conversations and write messages. Then take real messages from phone calls at home or work.

CHAPTER 6

The Community

COMPETENCIES: Understanding community services and information
Using checking accounts
Using the postal service

SPELLING: The consonants *b, p, v, f, w, wh*

GRAMMAR FOCUS: The future

PART ONE / READ AND UNDERSTAND

● Community Services and Information

Community Services

Most communities (cities, parts of cities, counties, and towns) offer many different kinds of services. Usually federal, state, county, or city governments run the service organizations and agencies, but some are private.

Some of the organizations, such as the Alcoholism Hotline, the Child Abuse Hotline, or the Rape Hotline, give help to people in emergencies or serious situations. Callers don't have to give their names to hotline operators. People in need can get advice by telephone. They can also get the names of and information about other helpful local agencies, like health and counseling services, the legal aid society, and the fair housing commission.

Other kinds of organizations offer information and services for daily life. Callers can find out about transportation, employment, education, recreation, marriage, government, etc.

You'll find the telephone numbers of community service agencies in the local telephone book. Sometimes there is a directory of community services in a special section. You can also find some of them in the list of city, county, and federal government offices at the beginning of the white pages. Local information (dial 411) will have the numbers, too. Usually "800 numbers" are not local, but you can call them for free.

A. Are these sentences true? Answer *yes* or *no*.

1. no_ Only communities with a lot of money can offer services. In poor cities, community services are all private.

2. ____ Some services are for people with serious problems, and some are for daily living.

3. ____ Alcoholism, child abuse, and rape are examples of serious situations.

4. ____ Hotline operators ask all callers their names. Then they call the police.

5. ____ Some examples of service agencies are counseling centers, legal aid organizations, and fair housing commissions.

6. ____ You can get the numbers of community service organizations from the telephone book or information.

*B. Answer these questions.

1. What community services do governments and cities in your country offer?

2. Do you use or get information from community services in your town or city? Which agencies or organizations?

Community Information Numbers

Airport 555-8847	Library 555-1983
Amtrak (trains) 1-800-555-7245	Newspapers
Bus Lines (Local) 555-1200	The Daily News 555-7111
Car Pooling 555-RIDE	Parks and
City Hall 555-8121	Recreation 555-9898
Department of Motor	Post Office 555-6721
Vehicles (DMV) 555-5321	Public School
Employment Services	District 555-7100
(State) 555-7000	Social Security
Fair Housing Commission 555-6945	Administration 555-2038
Immigration 555-2119	Time 555-1212
Income Tax	Weather 555-1212
Federal (IRS) 989-0111	
State 1-800-852-5711	Hotlines
Information	
Local 411	Battered Women 555-1234
Long Distance ...... 1-area code-	Suicide Prevention 555-4321
555-1212	Drug Abuse 555-2341

____ **C.** **Read the questions. Write the telephone numbers from the above list on the lines.**

What number can you call for information about

1. planes? _555-8847_

2. city bus schedules? _____

3. a driver's license? _____

4. jobs? _____

5. books and magazines? _____

6. U.S. income tax forms? _____

7. local schools? _____

8. postage rates? _____

9. a Social Security number? _____

10. the weather tomorrow? _____

D. Read the problems and situations. Who can you call about them? Write the names of the organizations or agencies from page 78.

1. You're going to take a train trip, and you need to know the schedule.

   Amtrak

2. You want to drive to and from work with other people.

3. You want information about local government services.

4. An apartment manager won't rent to you because you're from another country.

5. Your relatives are going to live in this country, but they have problems with their visas.

6. You're going to place an ad in a local newspaper.

7. You're going to sign up for a swimming class at a city park.

8. You can't find your watch, and your clocks are wrong.

9. You find drugs and alcohol in your son's room. You're very worried.

*E. What services in the list on page 78 interest you? Write them here. Then copy their numbers from your local telephone book.

Service	Number
1.	
2.	

PART TWO / INFORMATION

● Checking Accounts ● Postal Service

Checking Accounts

Most North American families have at least one checking account at a bank or a savings and loan institution. You can pay bills with checks, and in most situations they are safer than cash. Most people mail checks instead of money and deposit their paychecks directly into their accounts.

For a deposit to a checking account, in person or by mail, you fill out a deposit slip.

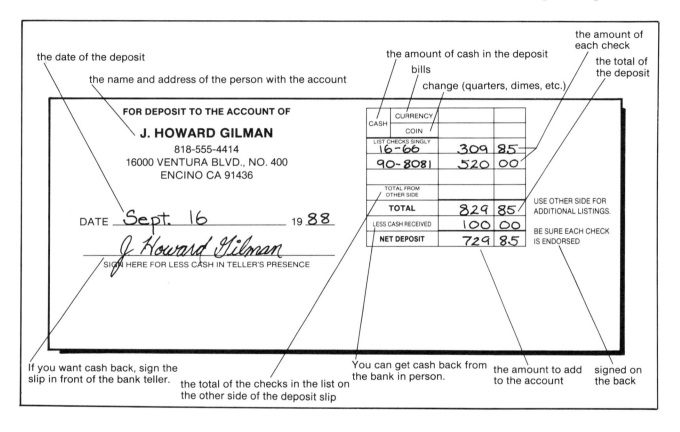

A. Find the information in the deposit slip. Answer the questions.

1. Who's the person with the account? _____

2. Is the person going to deposit any cash? _____

3. How many checks will he deposit? _____ What's their total? _____

4. How much cash does he want back from the bank? _____

5. What's the total deposit to the account? _____

B. Fill out the deposit slips with this information. Use today's date.

1. You're going to deposit $75 in bills (and no change) and checks for these amounts: $90.85 (number 11-66), $300.00 (number 90-711), and $550.11 (number 16-70). You're not going to get any cash back from the bank.

FOR DEPOSIT TO THE ACCOUNT OF

CASH	CURRENCY	75	00
	COIN		
LIST CHECKS SINGLY			
TOTAL FROM OTHER SIDE			
TOTAL			
LESS CASH RECEIVED			
NET DEPOSIT			

DATE _____ 19 ____

_____
SIGN HERE FOR LESS CASH IN TELLER'S PRESENCE

USE OTHER SIDE FOR ADDITIONAL LISTINGS.

BE SURE EACH CHECK IS ENDORSED

2. You're going to deposit this cash and these checks.

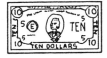   

FOR DEPOSIT TO THE ACCOUNT OF

CASH	CURRENCY		
	COIN		
LIST CHECKS SINGLY			
TOTAL FROM OTHER SIDE			
TOTAL			
LESS CASH RECEIVED			
NET DEPOSIT			

DATE _____ 19 ____

_____
SIGN HERE FOR LESS CASH IN TELLER'S PRESENCE

USE OTHER SIDE FOR ADDITIONAL LISTINGS.

BE SURE EACH CHECK IS ENDORSED

Your bank will send you a statement of your checking account every month.

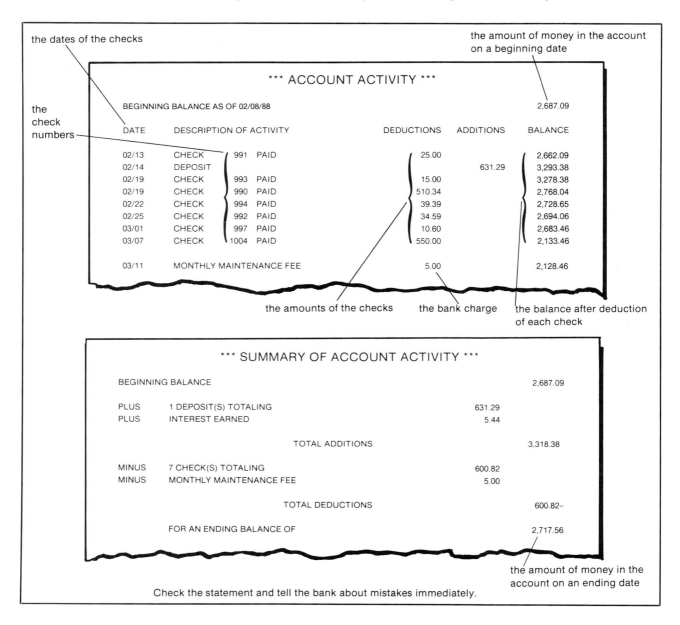

the dates of the checks

the amount of money in the account on a beginning date

the check numbers

*** ACCOUNT ACTIVITY ***

BEGINNING BALANCE AS OF 02/08/88   2,687.09

DATE	DESCRIPTION OF ACTIVITY			DEDUCTIONS	ADDITIONS	BALANCE
02/13	CHECK	991	PAID	25.00		2,662.09
02/14	DEPOSIT				631.29	3,293.38
02/19	CHECK	993	PAID	15.00		3,278.38
02/19	CHECK	990	PAID	510.34		2,768.04
02/22	CHECK	994	PAID	39.39		2,728.65
02/25	CHECK	992	PAID	34.59		2,694.06
03/01	CHECK	997	PAID	10.60		2,683.46
03/07	CHECK	1004	PAID	550.00		2,133.46
03/11	MONTHLY MAINTENANCE FEE			5.00		2,128.46

the amounts of the checks   the bank charge   the balance after deduction of each check

*** SUMMARY OF ACCOUNT ACTIVITY ***

BEGINNING BALANCE			2,687.09
PLUS	1 DEPOSIT(S) TOTALING	631.29	
PLUS	INTEREST EARNED	5.44	
	TOTAL ADDITIONS		3,318.38
MINUS	7 CHECK(S) TOTALING	600.82	
MINUS	MONTHLY MAINTENANCE FEE	5.00	
	TOTAL DEDUCTIONS		600.82–
	FOR AN ENDING BALANCE OF		2,717.56

the amount of money in the account on an ending date

Check the statement and tell the bank about mistakes immediately.

C. Find the information in the bank statement. Write it on the lines.

1. the beginning date of the statement ___*2/8/88*___

   the ending date _____

2. the number of deposits _____ the number of checks _____

3. the beginning balance _____ the ending balance _____

The United States Postal Service

The United States postal service offers different kinds of services. You'll pay the highest postage rates for first class mail. Postcards, letters, and small packages usually go first class. You can send newspapers, books, and magazines at special cheaper rates, and packages can go parcel post.

You can register and insure valuable or important mail. The receiver of registered mail has to sign a receipt for it. Express mail service will deliver your letter or package overnight. You can send mail overseas by air or surface mail.

Be sure to address all letters and packages correctly and completely in clear handwriting.

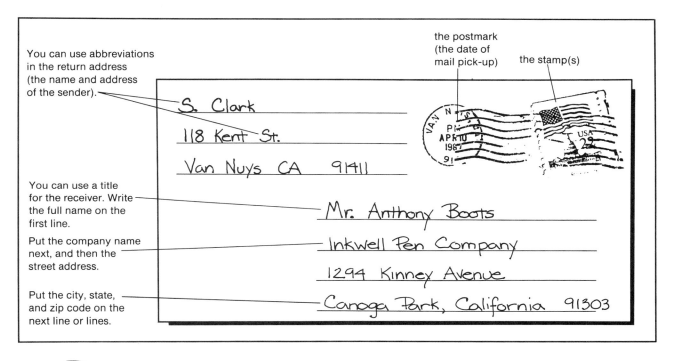

You can use abbreviations in the return address (the name and address of the sender).

the postmark (the date of mail pick-up)

the stamp(s)

S. Clark
118 Kent St.
Van Nuys CA 91411

You can use a title for the receiver. Write the full name on the first line.

Put the company name next, and then the street address.

Put the city, state, and zip code on the next line or lines.

Mr. Anthony Boots
Inkwell Pen Company
1294 Kinney Avenue
Canoga Park, California 91303

D. Circle the letter of the answer to each question.

1. How can you send most letters and postcards in North America?
   a. first class   **b.** second class   **c.** parcel post   **d.** insured

2. How can you protect valuable or important mail?
   a. Send it surface mail.   **b.** Register and insure it.
   c. Put it in a magazine.   **d.** Deliver it overnight.

3. Where do you put the stamp or stamps on an envelope?
   a. in the lower left-hand corner   **b.** in the middle
   c. in the upper right-hand corner   **d.** at the bottom

4. What goes in the upper left-hand corner of an envelope?
   a. the date   **b.** the return address
   c. the postmark   **d.** the receiver

E.   Read the information, fill out the forms, and address the envelope.

1. This express mail package from you is for the Microgood Company, 1111 Industry Drive, Charlotte, North Carolina 28212.

PRESS HARD
YOU ARE MAKING FOUR COPIES

FROM:

TO:

*POST OFFICE
TO ADDRESSEE*

The receiver will sign for the package.

° Signature is required upon delivery.
° Claims for delay, loss or damage must be made within 90 days. Claim forms may be obtained at the post office of mailing.
° This receipt must be presented when a claim is filed.

Bring it back to the post office if there's a problem.

EXPRESS MAIL SERVICE

Customer Receipt

2. This registered letter from you is worth $50. You buy insurance for it. It's to Phil True, 6578 Cheeter Place, Westwood, Massachusetts 02090.

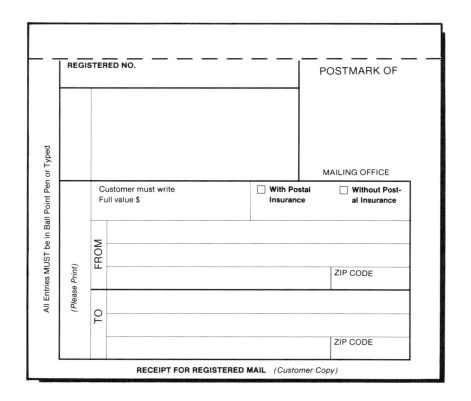

All Entries MUST be in Ball Point Pen or Typed

REGISTERED NO.

POSTMARK OF

MAILING OFFICE

(Please Print)

Customer must write Full value $

☐ **With Postal Insurance**   ☐ **Without Postal Insurance**

FROM

ZIP CODE

TO

ZIP CODE

RECEIPT FOR REGISTERED MAIL   *(Customer Copy)*

3. This letter from you is to a relative or friend in another country.

4. You're going to send this package today. There are two $25 shirts, $40 shoes, and a $15 book in it. If the post office can't deliver it, you want it back. It weighs 5 pounds and 10 ounces. If the post office can't deliver the packages, you have to pay postage for their return.

PARCEL POST CUSTOMS DECLARATION — UNITED STATES OF AMERICA			
SENDER'S INSTRUCTIONS	QTY	DETAILED LIST OF CONTENTS (Type or use Ballpoint Pen)	VALUE (U.S. $)
If item is undeliverable: ☐ Return to sender. (Sender guarantees return charges.) ☐ Forward to: _____ _____ ☐ Abandon.			
Signature Date			
Weight lbs. ozs.	Postage $		

PS Form 2966-A, July 1981

F. **Bring to class other bank and post office forms. Talk about them and then fill them out.

PART THREE / SPELLING

● The Consonants *b, p, v, f, w, wh*

Letters	b		p		v	
Examples	<u>b</u>aseball	<u>b</u>ottom	<u>p</u>ackage	a<u>pp</u>le	<u>v</u>ery	o<u>v</u>er
	<u>b</u>usiness	jo<u>b</u>	<u>p</u>ost	sto<u>p</u>	<u>V</u>ictor	lo<u>v</u>e

Letters	f		w		wh	
Examples	<u>f</u>ood	o<u>f</u>fice	<u>w</u>aiter	<u>w</u>eek	<u>wh</u>at	<u>wh</u>ere
	<u>f</u>ill	sa<u>f</u>e	<u>w</u>orld	<u>w</u>e	<u>wh</u>y	<u>wh</u>en

At the beginning of a syllable, the letter *w* makes a consonant sound. At the end, it is part of the vowel sound (Example: <u>row</u>).

A. Listen to the sentences. Write the consonant letters.

b	p	v

1. Give __ack my __ank

   __ook.

2. I'll __ay for the

   a____le __ie.

3. Ste__en lo__es

   tele__ision.

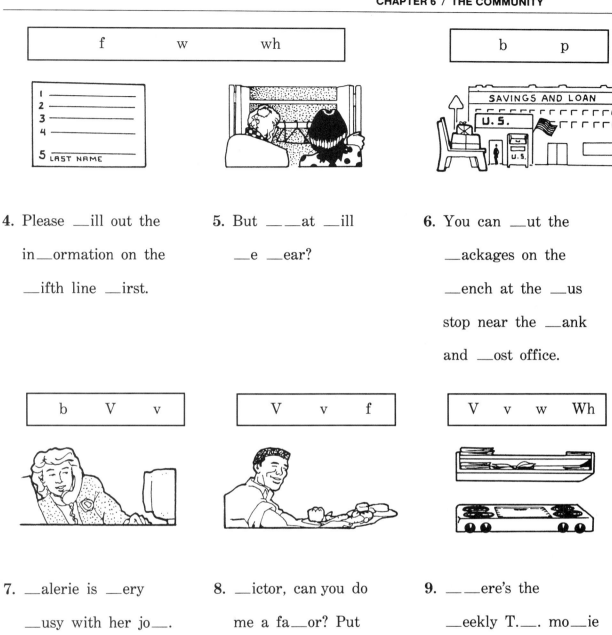

| f   w   wh |

| b   p |

4. Please __ill out the in__ormation on the __ifth line __irst.

5. But __ __at __ill __e __ear?

6. You can __ut the __ackages on the __ench at the __us stop near the __ank and __ost office.

| b   V   v |

| V   v   f |

| V   v   w   Wh |

7. __alerie is __ery __usy with her jo__. Is this her __oyfriend, Ste__en?

8. __ictor, can you do me a fa__or? Put the __egetables and the other __ood here.

9. __ __ere's the __eekly T.__. mo__ie program? Is it on the shel__es o__er the sto__e?

_____ **B.** **Now read the above sentences aloud.**

_____ ***C.*** **Write other words with the letters _b, p, v, f, w,_ and _wh_.**
Tell the meanings.

PART FOUR / READ AND WRITE

● Checks and Checkbook Registers

A Check

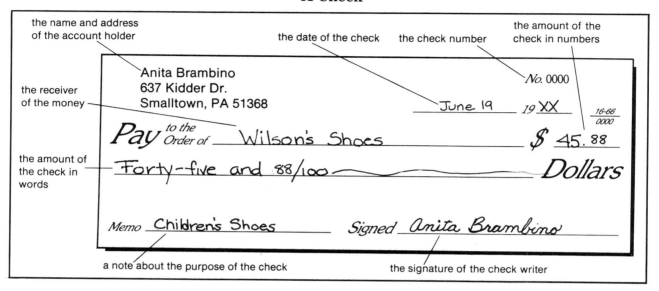

the name and address of the account holder

the date of the check

the check number

the amount of the check in numbers

the receiver of the money

the amount of the check in words

Anita Brambino
637 Kidder Dr.
Smalltown, PA 51368

No. 0000

June 19   19 XX   16-66/0000

Pay to the Order of   Wilson's Shoes $ 45.88

Forty-five and 88/100   Dollars

Memo Children's Shoes   Signed Anita Brambino

a note about the purpose of the check

the signature of the check writer

A. Read the bills. Write checks for them.

1. U.S. Postmaster

SANTA MONICA, CA
SEP 17 1989
USPO

40.83 *

No. 0000

Sept. 17 19____   16-66/0000

Pay to the Order of _____ $ _____

_____   Dollars

Memo _____   Signed _____

2. Atlantic Telephone Company

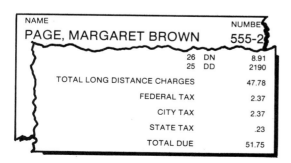

NAME	NUMBER
PAGE, MARGARET BROWN	555-2

26	DN	8.91
25	DD	2190
TOTAL LONG DISTANCE CHARGES		47.78
FEDERAL TAX		2.37
CITY TAX		2.37
STATE TAX		.23
TOTAL DUE		51.75

No. 0000

_____ 19____   16-66/0000

Pay to the Order of _____ $ _____

_____   Dollars

Memo _____   Signed _____

A Checkbook Register

You can keep a record of your deposits and checks in your checkbook register. You can check your bank statement against your record.

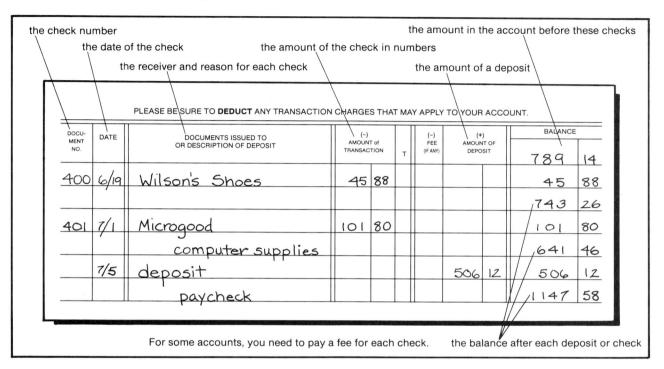

the check number

the date of the check

the receiver and reason for each check

the amount of the check in numbers

the amount in the account before these checks

the amount of a deposit

PLEASE BE SURE TO **DEDUCT** ANY TRANSACTION CHARGES THAT MAY APPLY TO YOUR ACCOUNT.

DOCU-MENT NO.	DATE	DOCUMENTS ISSUED TO OR DESCRIPTION OF DEPOSIT	(−) AMOUNT of TRANSACTION	T	(−) FEE (IF ANY)	(+) AMOUNT OF DEPOSIT	BALANCE	
							789	14
400	6/19	Wilson's Shoes	45 88				45	88
							743	26
401	7/1	Microgood	101 80				101	80
		computer supplies					641	46
	7/5	deposit				506 12	506	12
		paycheck					1147	58

For some accounts, you need to pay a fee for each check.   the balance after each deposit or check

B. **Fill in this checkbook register page with the information from the checks on page 88.**

PLEASE BE SURE TO **DEDUCT** ANY TRANSACTION CHARGES THAT MAY APPLY TO YOUR ACCOUNT.

DOCU-MENT NO.	DATE	DOCUMENTS ISSUED TO OR DESCRIPTION OF DEPOSIT	(−) AMOUNT of TRANSACTION	T	(−) FEE (IF ANY)	(+) AMOUNT OF DEPOSIT	BALANCE	

C. **Write checks of your own for real bills. Write the information in your checkbook register. Compare your register with the monthly bank statement. Are both correct?

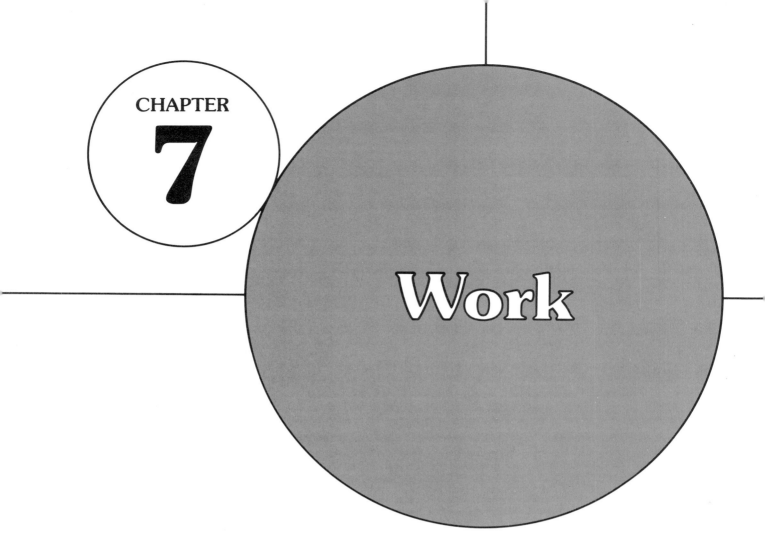

CHAPTER 7

Work

COMPETENCIES: Knowing things to do to get a job
Understanding newspaper ads for jobs
Using social security numbers and forms
Understanding and filling out job applications
Using alphabetical order

SPELLING: The vowels *o, aw, a, au, u, oo, oy, oi, ou, ow*
The endings -(e)d and -(e)r

GRAMMAR FOCUS: The past
The comparative

PART ONE / READ AND UNDERSTAND

● Things to Do to Get a Job ● Newspaper Ads for Jobs

Looking for a Job

You need skills to work. You also need skills to get a job. First, you have to find out about the openings for available positions. Many people learn about jobs from their friends, classmates, and relatives. Some look at notices on school bulletin boards and talk to job counselors. You can also look for jobs and fill out forms at the state employment office. Some people go there regularly. Private employment agencies and services also offer help. Agencies usually pay fees to employers, but some services receive part of their applicants' salaries for their first year of work at a new job. You can also answer classified ads for employment. Look in the local newspaper under the job titles for your kind of work.

To apply for most jobs, you have to fill out application forms. Some job applications ask for a personal fact sheet or resume. To set up interviews, you usually have to call up companies or write letters of application. Job interview skills are very important.

A. Check the places to look for jobs.

1. ✓ on a school bulletin board

2. ___ at the post office

3. ___ at the IRS or DMV

4. ___ at the state employment office

5. ___ at a private employment agency or service

6. ___ at the Social Security Administration

7. ___ at the Fair Housing Commission

8. ___ in the classified ads of a local newspaper

B. Check the important things to do to get a job.

1. ___ apply for carpooling

2. ___ fill out an application

3. ___ set up an interview

4. ___ open a checking account

5. ___ write a personal fact sheet or resume

6. ___ order an income-tax form

7. ___ send a registered letter

8. ___ learn interview skills

Abbreviations in Job Ads

Newspapers use abbreviations and symbols in ads.

Examples   bene. or bnft. = benefits   exp'd or exper'd = experienced

---

C. Read the words. Write them after the abbreviations and symbols.

appointment	experience(d)	paid	salary
before	graduate	plus	temporary
benefits	immediate	preferred	vacation
company	male / female	references	week

1. temp. = ~~temporary~~

2. M / F = _____

3. wk. = _____

4. ref. = _____

5. grad. = _____

6. vac. = _____

7. appt. = _____

8. bene. = _____

9. co. = _____

10. immed. = _____

11. bef. = _____

12. pd. = _____

13. + = _____

14. pref'd = _____

15. sal. = _____

16. exper'd = _____

excellent	nights	opportunity	words per minute
evenings	per week	qualifications	per year
per hour	percent	thousand	and
high school	manager	required	with

17. mgr. = _____

18. h.s. = _____

19. w/ = _____

20. /wk. = _____

21. K = _____

22. /yr. = _____

23. & = _____

24. % = _____

25. req'd = _____

26. xlnt. = _____

27. eves. = _____

28. nites = _____

29. /hr. = _____

30. oppor. = _____

31. w.p.m. = _____

32. qual. = _____

Classified Job Ads

```
Sales
Flower shop needs exper'd
salespeople, h.s. grads and
some college pref'd. Good
sal. + bene. package. Call
personnel mgr. for interview
appt. bef. 5:00.        555-8881
```
A

```
Construction
Immed. openings for full-time
temp. workers M / F. Some exper.
req'd. $400/wk. + pd. vac. Send
fact sheet with ref. to
      The Mark Bauer Co.
      2216 Wood Ave.
```
B

```
Security
GUARD needed in hospital, eves.
and nites, 30 - 50 hrs./wk.
For appt., call Mr. Cure
at 555-4399 bef. 10:00.
```
C

```
Sewing Operators
Openings for exper'd and new
machine operators. Will train.
$5-6/hr. Apply in person.
      Mary Jane Co.
      5504 Silk St.
an equal oppor. employer M/F
```
D

```
Secretary/Receptionist
LEGAL TRAINEE $18 K/yr. You
can learn and make a high sal.
Bilingual pref'd. Type 70 w.p.m.
100% free.

ROYAL PERSONNEL SERVICES
16156 Golden Way 555-3000
eves. call 555-3212
```
E

```
Shipping and Receiving
CLERK wanted immed. Xlnt. pay
and bene. for right person.
Qual. 1 yr. exper. & driver's
license. Call mgr. at 555-3001
```
F

____ **D.** **What jobs can these people apply for? Write the letters of the ads**
A–F on the lines.

1. _E_ I have office skills, and I type very fast. I want to earn a lot of money and learn about law.

2. ____ My brother just graduated from high school, and he wants a full-time job. He has some sales experience.

3. ____ My husband goes to school in the daytime. He needs a job in the evening or at night. Maybe he can study at work.

4. ____ Our daughter worked in a store last year. She packed and sent out boxes and carried things. She has a car.

5. ____ My aunt stayed home and took care of the house, but now the family needs more money. She sewed clothes for her three children.

6. ____ My cousins are very strong, and they like physical work. They built their own house. They're going to move in a year, so they don't want permanent jobs.

____ ****E.** **Bring to class classified ads from the local newspaper. Write the**
abbreviations on the board and tell the meanings. Talk about the ads.

PART TWO / INFORMATION

● Social Security Numbers and Forms ● Job Applications

Social Security

To work in the United States, you have to have a social security number. Every person has a different number, and you keep your number all your life. It is useful for identification even if you don't work.

In most jobs, employers take amounts of money for social security out of all the employees' paychecks. You pay this tax on all your salary and wages. Hopefully, the government will make social security payments to you at some time in your life.

To get a social security number, bring identification (a passport, a birth certificate, etc.) to the local social security office. Fill out an application. You will receive your card in the mail in a few weeks.

SOCIAL SECURITY ADMINISTRATION

SOCIAL SECURITY NUMBER CARD

Unless the requested information is provided, we may not be able to issue a Social Security Number. (20 CFR 422-103 (b)).

INSTRUCTIONS TO APPLICANT	You can type or print with pen. Do not use pencil.		
NAA	NAME FOR CARD First *Marta* Middle *Francisca*		Last *Melgar*
NAB **1** ONA	FULL NAME AT BIRTH (IF OTHER THAN ABOVE) First *Marta* Middle *Francisca*		Last *Balboa*
	OTHER NAME(S) USED		

STT 2 CTY

MAILING ADDRESS *2506 Elmhurst Blvd. #21*   (Street/Apt. No., P.O. Box#)

CITY *Chicago*   STATE *Illinois*   ZIP CODE *60625*

3

CITIZENSHIP (Check one only)

☐ a. U.S. citizen   ☐ c. Legal alien not allowed to work

☒ b. Legal alien allowed to work   ☐ d. Other

4

SEX   SEX

☐ Male

☒ Female

DOB **5**	DATE OF BIRTH MO. *2*	DAY *21*	YEAR *60*	AGE **6**	PRESENT AGE *28*	PLB **7**	PLACE OF BIRTH CITY *San Salvador*	STATE OR FOREIGN COUNTRY *El Salvador*
DOB **8**	MOTHER'S NAME AT HER BIRTH First *Ana*				Middle *Matilde*			Last *Salazar*
	FATHER'S NAME First *Juan*				Middle *Gabriel*			Last *Balboa*

DON **9**	TODAY'S DATE MONTH *4*	DAY *3*	YEAR *19XX*	**10**	Telephone number where we can reach you during the day HOME *555-3196*	OTHER

ASD **11**	YOUR SIGNATURE *Marta Francisca Melgar*	**12**	YOUR RELATIONSHIP TO PERSON IN ITEM 1 ☒ Self ☐ Other _____ (Specify)

A. Find the information in the social security application on page 94. Answer the questions.

1. What is the applicant's last name? _Melgar_

   Her maiden name? _____ Her mother's maiden name?

   _____ Does she have a middle name? _____

   Did she use any other names at work in the past? _____

2. Is she a U. S. citizen? _____ Can she work legally in the United States? _____

3. How old is she now? _____ Was she born in the United States? _____

4. Did she fill out the form herself? _____

B. Fill out this form with information about you.

SOCIAL SECURITY ADMINISTRATION								

SOCIAL SECURITY NUMBER CARD

Unless the requested information is provided, we may not be able to issue a Social Security Number. (20 CFR 422-103 (b)).

INSTRUCTIONS TO APPLICANT	You can type or print with pen. Do not use pencil.		

NAA	NAME FOR CARD	First	Middle	Last
NAB **1** ONA	FULL NAME AT BIRTH (IF OTHER THAN ABOVE)	First	Middle	Last
	OTHER NAME(S) USED			

STT **2** CTY	MAILING ADDRESS	(Street/Apt. No., P.O. Box#)	
	CITY	STATE	ZIP CODE

3	CITIZENSHIP (Check one only)		SEX **4**	SEX
	☐ a. U.S. citizen	☐ c. Legal alien not allowed to work		☐ Male
	☐ b. Legal alien allowed to work	☐ d. Other		☐ Female

DOB **5**	DATE OF BIRTH	MO.	DAY	YEAR	AGE **6**	PRESENT AGE	PLB **7**	PLACE OF BIRTH	CITY	STATE OR FOREIGN COUNTRY

DOB **8**	MOTHER'S NAME AT HER BIRTH	First	Middle	Last
	FATHER'S NAME	First	Middle	Last

DON **9**	TODAY'S DATE	MONTH	DAY	YEAR	**10**	Telephone number where we can reach you during the day	HOME	OTHER

ASD **11**	YOUR SIGNATURE	**12**	YOUR RELATIONSHIP TO PERSON IN ITEM 1
			☐ Self
			☐ Other _____ (Specify)

Job Applications

Job applications are very important. They have to be neat and correct. If there are mistakes, some employers will not want to interview the applicants. All of these parts of applications are wrong in some way.

A NAME ~~Terry D.~~ Davis, ~~Terry~~   TELEPHONE (314) 555-0606
       last   first

ADDRESS 240 Mayflower St. ~~St. Louis~~ CITY AND STATE St. Louis, MO

Education

B

Grammar School	Location		Dates	
Delmar Elementary	Trenton NJ		1972-80	
High School	Location		Dates	Main Subjects
University H.S.	Boston MA		1980-84	English, Languages
Trade / Vocational School	Location		Dates	Main Subjects

Do not write below this line.

Royal Business School

Work Experience (Put present or last job first.)

	Date (Month and Year)	Name and Location of Employer	Salary	Position	Reason for Leaving
C From	1980	Pia's Pizza	$	driver (delivery truck)	summer jobs
To	1981				
From	1984	McDougal's Hamburgers		counter	got better
To	1988	Los Angeles CA		person	job
From	1988	The Rose Restaurant		waiter	
To	now	Venice CA			

D References (Do not include relatives.)

NAME AND ADDRESS	RELATIONSHIP
1. Mr. Joe Dominick	uncle
2. Ms. Ana Ayala	sister

Do not write in this box.
Xlnt good fair
Language Ability   ☒   ☐   ☐

C. Write the letters of the application parts on the lines.

1. **B**   This applicant wrote information below the lines instead of on them, so she didn't have room for all the information.

2. _____   This application is messy because the applicant didn't read it first. She wrote her first name first and her city and state on the wrong line. Then she crossed out her mistakes.

3. ____ This applicant didn't read the instructions, so he put down his relatives as references. Also, he wrote in the box for the interviewer.

4. ____ This applicant put his job experience in the wrong order.

____ **D.** Fill out this job application with information about you.

NAME _____ TELEPHONE _____
last   first

ADDRESS _____ CITY AND STATE _____

Education

Grammar School	Location		Dates	
High School	Location		Dates	Main Subjects
Trade / Vocational School	Location		Dates	Main Subjects

Do not write below this line.

Work Experience (Put present or last job first.)

	Date (Month and Year)	Name and Location of Employer	Salary	Position	Reason for Leaving
From / To					
From / To					
From / To					

References (Do not include relatives.)

NAME AND ADDRESS   RELATIONSHIP

1. _____
2. _____

Do not write in this box.

Xlnt good fair

Language Ability ☐ ☐ ☐

****E.** Get job applications from local businesses. Talk about the information. Fill out the forms.

PART THREE / SPELLING

● The Vowels *o, aw, a, au, u, oo, oy, oi, ou, ow* ● The Endings *-(e)d* and *-(e)r*

Letters	o aw	a au	u oo	oy oi	ou ow
Examples	cr<u>o</u>ss dr<u>aw</u>	t<u>a</u>lk la<u>u</u>ndry	p<u>u</u>t g<u>oo</u>d	empl<u>oy</u> n<u>oi</u>se	ar<u>ou</u>nd fl<u>ow</u>er

A. Listen to the words. Write the vowel letters.

| a   o   au   aw |

1.

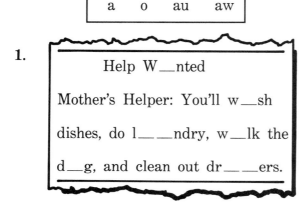

Help W__nted

Mother's Helper: You'll w__sh
dishes, do l____ndry, w__lk the
d__g, and clean out dr____ers.

| u   oo |

2.

Take a g____d l____k at this
ad for f__ll-time work on the
b__lletin board. I'll p__t it here.

| oy   oi |

3.

Phone Sales

Our empl____ees need good

telephone v____ces.

Ch____ce of hours. You'll

enj____ this job. Call for an

app____intment.

| ou   ow |

4.

H____ ab____t h____sework?
I have to go d____nt____n in
an h____r to buy fl____ers.

_____ ***B.** **Write other words with the letters *o, aw, a, au, u, oo, oy, oi, ou,* and *ow*. Tell the meanings.**

	Spelling	Past or Comparative Form
try	If a word ends in *-y* after a consonant,	tr**ied**
easy	change the *y* to *i* and add *-ed* or *-er*.	eas**ier**
stay	If a word ends in *-y* after a vowel,	stay**ed**
	just add *-ed* or *-er*.	grey**er**
stop	If a word ends in one consonant after	stop**ped**
big	one vowel, double the last consonant	big**ger**
hot	and add *-ed* or *-er*.	hot**ter**
like	If a word ends in *-e*, just add *-d* or *-r*.	like**d**
large		larg**er**
walk	Add *-ed* or *-er* to other words.	walk**ed**
quiet		quiet**er**

_____ **C.** **Write the *-(e)d* and *-(e)r* words on the lines.**

I <u>needed</u> a job, so I _____ to friends and relatives. I _____

1. need   2. talk   3. walk

around the business area, and I _____ in stores with "Help Wanted" signs. I

4. stop

_____ newspaper ads, and I _____ to learn about companies. My brother

5. study   6. try

_____ me. We _____ the telephone every day, and he _____

7. help   8. use   9. type

letters for me. And I _____ a lot.

10. worry

I got two job offers. Now I have to choose between jobs at a supermarket and a laundry.

The market is a ___bigger___ place than the laundry, and it's _____ . The pay
        11. big   **12.** quiet

is _____ too. But the employees seemed _____ at the laundry because the
   13. high   **14.** happy

boss was _____ . Of course, they were _____ too, and the work was
      15. friendly   **16.** busy

_____ . How will I choose?
17. hard

D. Now read the stories from C aloud.

PART FOUR / READ AND WRITE

● Alphabetical Order ● "Help Wanted" and "Job Wanted" Ads

Alphabetical Order

Employment ads in the newspaper are listed under job or business titles. These titles are in alphabetical order.

Alphabetize words according to the first letter. If more than one word begins with the same letter or letters, alphabetize them according to the first different letter.	ACCOUNTING BANKING CASHIER CLERICAL COLLECTION COMPUTERS CONSTRUCTION

A. Number the words in each group in alphabetical order 1-8.

1.	2.	3.
_2_ CARPENTER	___ CHILDCARE	___ PRINTING
___ INSURANCE	___ MEDICAL	___ RESTAURANT
___ DATA PROCESSING	___ DRESSMAKER	___ PROGRAMMER
___ EDUCATION	___ DRIVERS	___ PERSONNEL
___ LABORATORY	___ DENTAL	___ RETAIL
___ HOSPITAL	___ ELECTRICIAN	___ RECEPTIONIST
_1_ ADVERTISING	___ GENERAL OFFICE	___ SALES
___ FOOD	___ LEGAL	___ REAL ESTATE

Job Titles

How can you find the right classified ads for your job skills? Most skills can be useful in more than one kind of job. The job or business titles in the employment ads usually include more than one kind of position. For example, if you have experience as a medical assistant, you can look under the titles "Laboratory," "Hospital," "Dental," and "Medical." A bookkeeper can answer ads with the titles "Accountant," "Data Processing," "Clerical," and "General Office." You can use language skills and ability to work with people in "Education," "Personnel," "Sales," and many other areas.

B. Write one or more job titles from page 101 for these skills. (There can be many correct answers.)

1. teaching ability, interest in children   *education, childcare*

2. cooking ability _____

3. clerical skills _____

4. building skills _____

5. interest in health _____

6. ability to sell _____

7. good language ability _____

8. good math skills _____

**C. In alphabetical order, list other job and business titles from the local newspaper. Circle the titles for your job skills.

Classified Ads

There are many "Help Wanted" ads in the classified part of the newspaper. Companies place these ads to get job applicants. There are also a few "Jobs Wanted" ads. Applicants place these to get job offers.

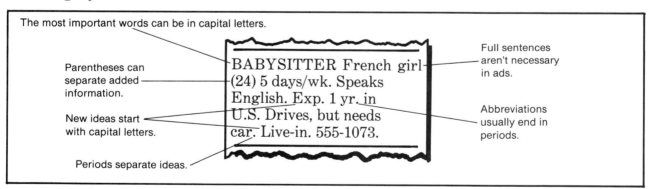

The most important words can be in capital letters.

Parentheses can separate added information.

New ideas start with capital letters.

Periods separate ideas.

BABYSITTER French girl (24) 5 days/wk. Speaks English. Exp. 1 yr. in U.S. Drives, but needs car. Live-in. 555-1073.

Full sentences aren't necessary in ads.

Abbreviations usually end in periods.

D. Add capital letters and punctuation to these ads.

1. secretary types 80 w p m
   xlnt refs needs temp
   part-time work call eves
   bef 9 p m 555-3421

2. handyman can do carpeting,
   electricity, plumbing can start
   immed h s grad w/ some
   college call jim at 555-8989

E. Cover the words under each line with paper. Listen, and write the ads. (There can be more than one way to write them.) Check your writing.

1. _____

MOTHER'S HELPER wants to

_____

live in your house, help

_____

w/ housework, take care of

_____

children. Some cooking.

_____

Call Kim at 555-1204.

2. _____

SALESCLERK needs temp.

_____

position in your small

_____

store or business. Xlnt.

_____

refs. 10 yrs. exp. Can work

_____

1 - 7 p.m.   555-2311

F. Write ads from these descriptions.

1. I'm a nurse's aide, and I can take care of an old or sick person and do some housekeeping in your home. I have 5 years' experience and excellent references. My name is Lisa, and you can call me evenings at 555-7766.

_____

_____

_____

_____

_____

_____

2. I want a security guard's job afternoons and evenings or nights, from 20 to 30 hours a week. I can do a handyman's work, too. I charge $8 an hour, and I can start immediately. My telephone number is 555-3420.

_____

_____

_____

_____

_____

_____

3. I can operate sewing machines. I can work part or full-time, days, evenings, or nights, 30 to 50 hours a week. I drive and have my own transportation. Call Len at 555-5431.

4. (your situation)

G. **Ask one or more classmates about their situations. Write "Jobs Wanted" ads for them.

CHAPTER

8

Shopping

COMPETENCIES: Using the telephone yellow pages
Using mail order catalogs and order forms
Reading and writing short business letters

SPELLING: The consonants *g, j, y, m, n, ng, qu, x*
The *-(e)st* ending

GRAMMAR FOCUS: Modal verbs
The superlative

PART ONE / READ AND UNDERSTAND

● The Telephone Yellow Pages

Index to the Telephone Yellow Pages

You might want to begin your shopping in the local telephone book. If you know the names of stores, you can look up their addresses and telephone numbers in the white pages. In the yellow pages, you will see ads, names, addresses, and telephone numbers under headings in alphabetical order. You can call stores and businesses for information. Retail stores sell things to the public, and wholesale dealers sell to stores and customers in large amounts.

The index to the yellow pages lists headings and their page numbers. Some headings will refer you to other headings.

Index

Appliances
Household - Major 26
See also Electrical Appliances

Appliances
Household - Small 237
See Electric Appliances - Small-
Dealers 237

Baby Shops 107
See also
Baby Carriages and Strollers
.... 107

Toys - Retail 659

Beds - Rental 122
See also
Waterbeds - Retail 695

Book Dealers - Retail 130
Book Dealers - Used and Rare
.... 131

Boy's Clothing - Retail 133

Children's Clothing 159

Clothing - Boy's
See Men's Clothing - Retail
.... 392

Clothing - Men's
See Men's Clothing - Retail 392

Clothing - Retail 174

Clothing - Used 174

Dresses - Retail 233
See also
Women's Clothing - 703

Fabric Shops 255

Furniture Dealers - New 279

Furniture Dealers - Used 282

Furniture - Office
See Office Furniture Dealers
.... 422

Furniture Repairing and
Refinishing 283

Furniture - Unfinished 284

Luggage - Repairing 377

Luggage - Retail 377

Men's Clothing - Retail 392

Suits
See Men's Clothing - Retail
.... 392

T-Shirts 634

Toys - Retail 659

A. Find the information in the index. Write it on the lines.

1. the page number for big household appliances _26_

   for stores with small electric appliances _____

   for renting beds _____   for sales of office furniture _____

   for furniture repair shops _____

2. the headings for things for babies _____

   _____ for clothing for men _____

   for books _____   _____

3. the pages for kinds of clothing stores _____ _____ _____ _____

   _____ _____

_____ ***B.** **Now ask and answer questions about the index to the yellow pages on page 106.**

Page Headings

At the top of each page in the telephone book, there are words from the first and last headings. Use these words to find alphabetical listings quickly.

A	APARTMENTS - AUTOMOBILE	64	**F**	FUR - GASOLINE	278
B	BABY - BAKERS	107	**G**	GIFTS - GIRLS	288
B	BEAUTY - BEDS	122	**H**	HAIR - HEALTH	301
B	BOAT - BOOKKEEPING	132	**J**	JEANS - KITCHEN	333
B	BOXES - BUILDING	134	**L**	LAMPS - MACHINE	364
C	CAR - CARPET	154	**M**	MAGAZINES - MUSIC	379
C	CLEANERS - CLOTHING	171	**N**	NEWSPAPERS - OFFICE	420
C	COMPUTERS - COPYING	185	**P**	PLUMBING - SALES	490
D	DELIVERY - DENTISTS	209	**S**	SCHOOLS - SHEET	511
D	DOGS - DRUG	224	**T**	TAX - TRAVEL	628
E	EXERCISE - FAMILY	254	**W**	WINDOWS - YARD	700

_____ **C.** **Where can you find listings for these things? Write the above page numbers.**

1. _64_ Appliances - Household

2. ____ Baby Shops

3. ____ Beds - Retail

4. ____ Book Dealers - Used

5. ____ Carpenters

6. ____ Clocks - Dealers

7. ____ Doors

8. ____ Driving Schools

9. ____ Furniture - Repairing

10. ____ Hardware Stores

11. ____ Jewelers

12. ____ Luggage - Retail

13. ____ Marriage Counselors

14. ____ Movers

15. ____ Office Furniture

16. ____ Quilts

17. ____ Television

18. ____ X-Ray Laboratories

D. What things do you want to buy? List five of them. Where can you find them? List the headings and the page numbers from the local yellow pages.

Item	Headings	Page
1. _____	_____ - _____	_____
2. _____	_____ - _____	_____
3. _____	_____ - _____	_____
4. _____	_____ - _____	_____
5. _____	_____ - _____	_____

Ads from the Yellow Pages

A

—BIG MAN'S SHOP—
Complete Selection to Size 54
Suits • Sport Coats • Slacks
Jackets • Shoes • Sweaters
Shirts • Work Clothes
Most Major Credit Cards
Free Parking
1069 Fairview   555-4480

B

JIMMY'S SMALL AND SHORT
Fine Clothing for
the Small and Short Man
Most Major Brands
We accept Mastercard and Visa.
16000 Oak Dr.   **555-5433**

C

BOB BROWN'S DESIGNER CLOTHING
FOR MEN

Mon. - Sat. 10 a.m. - 6 p.m.
12234 S. Main St.   **555-5645**
Low, low discount prices

D

SUGAR & SPICE
Selection of Used Clothing
Infants to Teens
Maternity Clothes
Play Area for Children
12300 W. Pine St.   **555-9871**

E

BABY TALK
Clothing for Sizes to 6X
All Cotton Clothing

Large Selection of Baby Toys
76 Westside Mall   **555-0089**

F

CLAIR BARGAIN CENTER
Best Prices on the East Side
Large Selection of:
* Used Furniture • Clothing
   • Lamps • Tools
   • Appliances • Shoes
   • Housewares • Books
   • Office Equipment • Toys
DOLLAR A BAG CLOTHING SALES
Open Mon., Wed., Sat. 9-5
Donations Accepted.
Call 555-9000 for Pick-Up.

E. Write the letters of the ads *A–F* on the lines.

1. _B_   Do you want major brands of clothing for men in small sizes? You can use credit cards at this store.

2. ____   This store sells many kinds of clothing for men in large sizes. You don't have to pay for parking.

3. ____   Would you like designer clothing at a discount? This is a men's store.

4. ____   This store sells only things for infants and babies. What would you like?

5. ____   You may find something nice for your children at this place. They might want to play here, too.

6. ____   You ought to get good bargains on clothing and things for the house at this store. You can donate your old things to them, too.

**F. Before your next shopping trip, look at the listings and ads in the yellow pages. Try a new store.

PART TWO / INFORMATION

● Mail Order Catalogs and Order Forms

Mail Order

You might want to shop by mail. You can fill out forms to order items from mail order catalogs, and you can pay for them by check or credit card number. Mail order might be more convenient than shopping in stores. It could be more or less expensive. You ought to receive your order in two to six weeks. You can return items for any reason, and the company should refund your money, but you may have to pay for postage.

Parts of a Mail Order Catalog

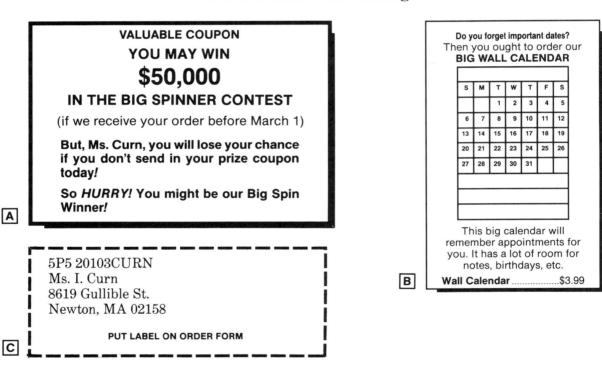

E

STOCK NO.	HOW MANY	NAME OF ITEM	(Size, Color)	PRICE EACH	TOTAL
W-513598	1	Super Pocket Knife		8.99	8.99
OW-165506	2	Towels—set		9.99	19.98

Shipping and Handling Chart
if your order is:

Up to $ 2.00 Add $ .70 $14.01 to $23.00 Add $3.50
$2.01 to $ 6.00 Add $1.50 $23.01 to $30.00 Add $3.95
$6.01 to $14.00 Add $2.65   Over $30.00 Add $4.45

MERCHANDISE TOTAL	28.97
POSTAGE	3.95
SUBTOTAL	32.92
STATE SALES TAX	1.74
TOTAL ENCLOSED	34.66

F

SURPRISE GIFT!

If you send in your order before March 15, you will receive a free gift!

A. Write the letters of the catalog parts on the lines.

1. _E_ an order form for items in a mail order catalog

2. ____ advertising for one item in the catalog

3. ____ the address label of the receiver of the catalog

4. ____ the part of the order form for credit card users

5. ____ a coupon for a possible prize in a contest

6. ____ an offer of a small free item for an early order

B. Are these sentences true? (Some ask for your opinion.) Write *yes* or *no* on the lines.

1. _yes_ You can shop through the mail if you have catalogs and order forms.

2. _____ You ought to always pay cash for the items in your order.

3. _____ Mail order is a bad idea because you can't return anything for a refund.

4. _____ Mail order items are always cheaper than things at the store because the company pays for postage.

5. _____ You can write your credit card number on an order form, but you shouldn't give it to other people.

6. _____ Companies might have contests and offer gifts to get more business.

7. _____ You should always send in contest forms because you might win a lot of money.

Descriptions from a Mail Order Catalog

Cancelled checks could save you money! So keep them safe. File has 12 parts — one for each month.
4″ x 8″

☐ **Check File** (W-985333) **$1.49**
Now only **$ .88**

"Four by eight inches" is the size.

The Super Pocket Knife!

To meet all kinds of emergencies. So much in one knife.

☐ **Super Pocket Knife**
(W-513598) **$8.99**

Never write another return address!
500 labels with your name and full address.
For all envelopes, books, checks.
White with black print. Write name, full address, and zip code number — 3 lines.

☐ **500 labels**
(DW-725465) *$1.19* Now **$ .88**

Lifetime Address Books

Don't cross out old addresses! To make a change, pull out an old card and put in a new one. Names are always in alphabetical order, A-Z. Includes 100 cards with room for name, address, phone.

Pocket size, 3″ x 5″. Desk size for home or office: 5″ x 7″.
Refill for pocket size has 50 cards. Refill for desk size has 100.

☐ **Pocket Address Book**
(W-741041) *$1.99* Now **$ .99**
☐ **Refills for Pocket Size**
(W-741124) *$ .79* Now **$ .36**
☐ **Desk Address Book**
(W-741207) *$3.99* Now **$1.99**
☐ **Refills for Desk Size**
(W-741389) *$ .99* Now **$ .49**

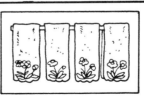

Flower towels are 100% white cotton.
Machine washable. Set of 4, each 14″ x 22″.

☐ **Towels** (OW-165506) **1 set** *$9.99*

C. Choose items from the catalog on page 112. Read the notes and fill out the order form.

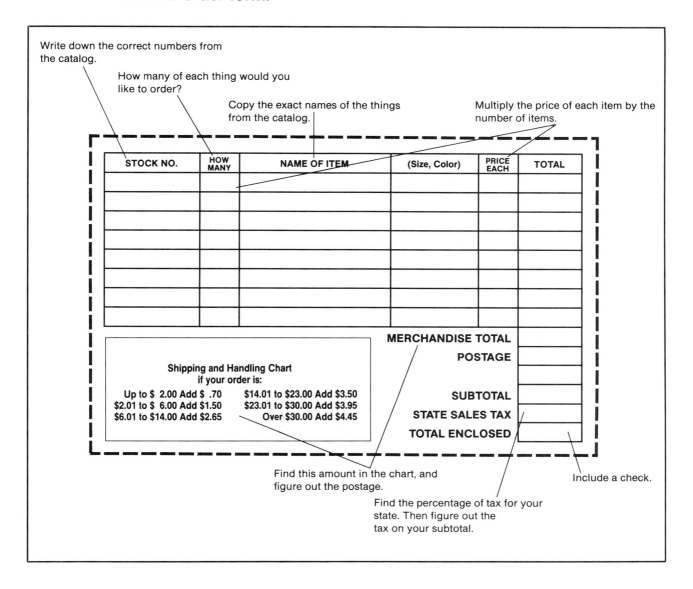

Write down the correct numbers from the catalog.

How many of each thing would you like to order?

Copy the exact names of the things from the catalog.

Multiply the price of each item by the number of items.

STOCK NO.	HOW MANY	NAME OF ITEM	(Size, Color)	PRICE EACH	TOTAL

MERCHANDISE TOTAL

POSTAGE

Shipping and Handling Chart
if your order is:

Up to $ 2.00 Add $ .70	$14.01 to $23.00 Add $3.50
$2.01 to $ 6.00 Add $1.50	$23.01 to $30.00 Add $3.95
$6.01 to $14.00 Add $2.65	Over $30.00 Add $4.45

SUBTOTAL

STATE SALES TAX

TOTAL ENCLOSED

Find this amount in the chart, and figure out the postage.

Include a check.

Find the percentage of tax for your state. Then figure out the tax on your subtotal.

**D. Bring mail-order catalogs to class. Talk about them. Fill out an order form.

PART THREE / SPELLING

● The Consonants *g, j, y, m, n, ng, qu, x* ● The *-(e)st* Ending

Spelling	Examples	
For the "g" sound, use the letter *g* in most words.	**g**et	bar**g**ain
For the "j" sound, use *g* only before *e, i,* and *y* in some words and before *e* at the end of all syllables. Use *j* in most words.	**G**erman refri**g**erator **j**acket	mana**g**er **j**eans
The letter *y* is a consonant at the beginning of syllables. At the end, it is part of the vowel sound.	**y**ear mone**y** pa**y**ment	**y**ou bu**y**

A. Listen to the words and write the consonant letters.

G   g

1.   __ood bar__ains at

__ary's __ift Shop!

__et a catalo__.

J   j   g

2.   Lar__e Sale at __immy's!

__ackets and __eans   Ma__or appliances!

for all a__es!   Refri__erators!

Y   y

3. __ou __oung people will love

these __ellow __ard chairs.

J   j   G   g   y

4. Do __ou need a __ob? __ack's

__ara__e pays __ood wa__es -

$18,000 a __ear!

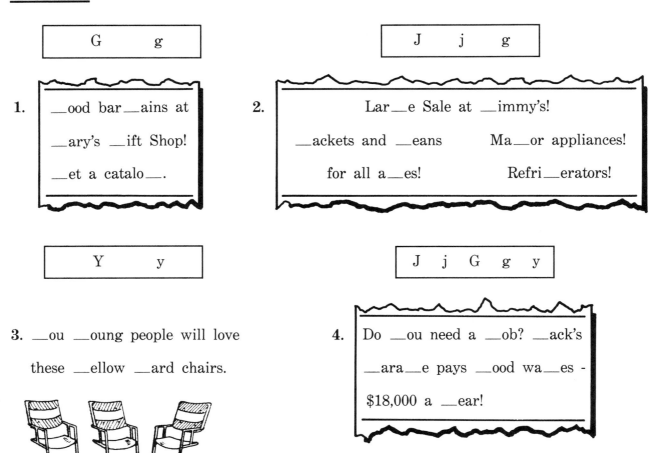

Spelling	Examples	
For the "m" sound, use the letter *m* in all words.	<u>m</u>aybe	ite<u>m</u>
For the "n" sound, use the letter *n* in all words.	<u>n</u>ice	fu<u>nn</u>y
For the "ng" sound, use *n* before *k*. Use *ng* at at the end of syllables.	tha<u>n</u>k	thi<u>ng</u>
Always use the letter *u* after *q*.	<u>qu</u>ick	<u>qu</u>iet
The letter *x* spells two sounds together.	ta<u>x</u>	e<u>x</u>act

B. Listen to the words and write the consonant letters.

1. __aybe I'll __ake e__ough __oney to buy so__e __ew __usic.

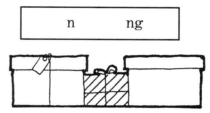

2. I thi__k I'll bri____ some __ice thi____s home from the shoppi____ ce__ter.

3. These bo__es of e____ipment cost e__actly si__ hundred si__ty dollars plus ta__.

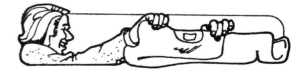

4. __ay I ____ickly show you some __en's and wo__e__'s e__tra lo____ clothi____?

C. Now read the above sentences aloud.

*D.

Write other words with the letters _g_, _j_, _y_, _m_, _n_, _ng_, _qu_, and _x_. Tell the meanings.

		Spelling	-(_e_)_st_ Form
pretty easy		If a word ends in -_y_ after a consonant, change the _y_ to _i_ and add -_est_.	prett**iest** eas**iest**
big		If a word ends in one consonant after one vowel, double the last consonant and add -_est_.	big**gest**
large		If a word ends in -_e_, just add -_st_.	large**st**
long		Add -_est_ to other words.	long**est**

E.

Write the -(_e_)_st_ words on the lines.

My favorite clothing store is Jimmy's Best Buys. Jimmy may

have the ___biggest___ selection of dresses, the _____ variety
1. big   2. large

of designer jeans, and the _____ choice of shirts and
3. wide

blouses at the _____ prices in the city. You can find the
4. low

_____ styles. Jimmy sells the _____ fabrics
5. funny   6. nice

with the _____ designs, and his sales clerks might be the
7. pretty

_____ of all.
8. friendly

PART FOUR / READ AND WRITE

● Short Business Letters

A Business Letter

If you order items by mail, you might need or want to write a letter about your order.

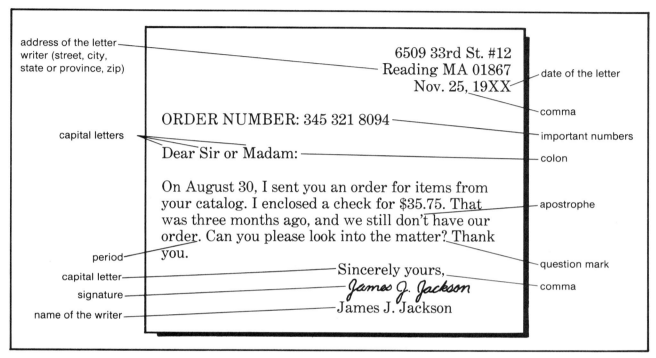

A. Change the small letters to capital letters. Write the colons, apostrophes, periods, and commas.

23045 broadway blvd
los angeles ca 90016
feb 16 19XX

ORDER NUMBER 675-45-811-02

dear sir or madam

five days ago i received an order from your company of
some slacks and two shirts the slacks are fine but the shirts
are the wrong size please accept their return and exchange
them for a larger size I d like to try size 16 thank you

sincerely yours

gene johnson

B. Cover the words under each line with paper. Listen and write. Then check your writing.

_____ 4389 New York Rd., Apt. 26

_____ Boston MA 02210

_____ Dec. 13, 19XX

_____
ORDER NUMBER: 543 98 7065 5

_____
Dear Sir or Madam:

_____
We received our order of luggage and toys a week ago.

_____
The luggage is O.K., but the toys don't work.

_____
Please accept their return and send us a refund of $21.98.

_____
We'd also like a new catalog. Thank you.

_____ Sincerely yours,

_____ (your name)

_____ C. Write a letter with this information.

The address of the writer is 45 Alma Place, Studio City, California 91604. His name is Gary Jones. The date of the letter is September 22 of this year. He received an order of clothing from a mail order company with the number 2221-76-1-2304. The shirt is the right size, but the company sent the wrong color. He'd like to exchange it for a blue and brown striped shirt of the same style.

_____

_____

_____

ORDER NUMBER: _____

Dear _____

_____

_____

_____

_____

_____

_____

_____

_____ **D. Do you order items by mail? If there is any problem, write a letter about it to the company.

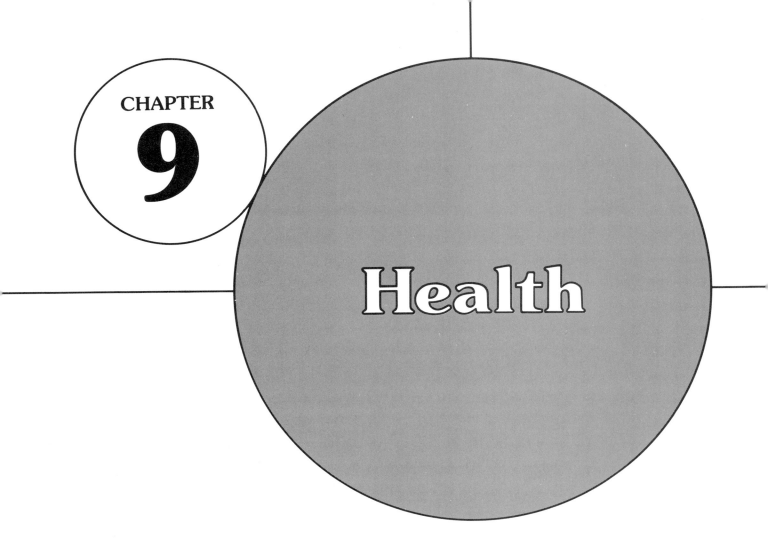

CHAPTER

9

Health

COMPETENCIES: Understanding kinds of health services
Reading medicine labels
Understanding medical insurance plans
Filling out insurance claim forms

SPELLING: The consonants *z, s, c, ch, tch, ck, f, ph, gh*
The *-ing* ending

GRAMMAR FOCUS: The continuous tenses

PART ONE / READ AND UNDERSTAND

● Kinds of Health Services ● Medicine Labels

Medical Care

Excellent health care is available in the United States and Canada, but it may be hard to find. It's usually very expensive, too, and medical costs are going up. You should probably find out about health services in your community now, before you get sick.

If you prefer to see a private doctor, you may want to ask friends and neighbors for some advice. Most people start with a general practitioner (G.P.) or internist. This family doctor advises them to see specialists, if necessary.

Most hospitals have outpatient departments or clinics. Anyone can get medical care there, and the costs may be lower than with private doctors. You might have to wait several hours at a clinic, and you may never see the same doctor twice. But it will probably have a lot of excellent equipment, some laboratories, and specialists in many kinds of medicine.

Most older people and many poor people are getting help with medical bills from the government. Many other people belong to group insurance plans through their places of employment. If you can't get any group health insurance, you may have to pay for coverage by a private company. Insurance policies differ in the cost and the amount of coverage. Very few plans pay all medical bills. You will want to get information about several plans before you decide on one.

A. Are these sentences true? Write yes or no.

1. no The costs of medical care are going down because insurance companies are paying for them.

2. ____ You can ask friends or neighbors to tell you the names of family doctors (G.P.s or internists).

3. ____ Only hospital patients can use the services of hospital clinics, laboratories, and specialists.

4. ____ You may have to wait a long time at outpatient clinics, but they're probably less expensive than private doctors.

5. ____ The government is helping to pay the medical fees for some patients.

6. ____ Private health insurance pays all doctors' bills, but group plans don't.

*B. Answer the questions.

1. Is health and medical care in your country better or worse than in the United States or Canada? Why?

2. What kinds of doctors and clinics are you going to in this country? Who (or what company) is paying the bills?

Medical Building Directory

Achoo, Albert, M.D.	Allergies	360
Bone, Barbara, M.D.	Orthopedics	302
Brown, Iris, M.D.	Opthalmology	430
F.L.U. Associates	Ear, Nose, and Throat	238
Hart, Gerald, M.D.	Cardiology	211
Head, Harold, M.D.	Psychiatry	418
Kidder, Karol, M.D.	Pediatrics	222
Inman, Carl, M.D.	Internal Medicine	436
Pie Medical Group	Podiatry	318
Skinner, Stanley, M.D.	Dermatology	322
Young, Yolanda, M.D.	Obstetrics and Gynecology	216
Zahn, Peter, D.D.S.	Dentistry	422

C. Where are these people going or waiting? Write the office numbers on the lines.

1. _216_ A pregnant woman is going to her doctor for a checkup.

2. _____ A father is taking his children to their doctor.

3. _____ Several people have an appointment for an eye examination.

4. _____ A woman with foot problems is waiting for her doctor.

5. _____ A teenager with a skin problem needs help and medicine.

6. _____ Some people with family problems are talking to a specialist in mental health.

7. _____ A man with a lot of back pain can't walk very well.

8. _____ A brother and sister with sore throats and earaches are seeing the doctor.

9. _____ Some people with allergies are looking for advice.

Medicine Labels

A

NITE-NITE MEDICINE FOR COLDS

relieves pain from sneezing, coughing, and sore throat.

ADULTS (12 years and over) 2 tablespoons at bedtime.
DON'T GIVE TO CHILDREN

B

REMEDEZE
PAIN RELIEF CREAM

for relief of pain from small injuries and sunburn

DIRECTIONS: Rub in gently on painful areas. DO NOT USE IN EYES.
WARNING: Keep this and all other medications out of reach of children.

C

Atton Pharmacy
34 Montana Ave. Santa Monica, CA

No. 762781   Dr. Davis

Phil Hurt   4/28/88

TAKE 1 CAPSULE 3 TIMES DAILY AS NEEDED FOR ITCHING.

DISCARD AFTER 8/89

BENADRYL CAPS 25 MG

D

BUYUM ASPIRIN

Fast relief of pain from headaches and fever.

Dosage: 2 tablets. Repeat after 4 hours, if necessary. Do not take more than 8 tablets in 24 hours.

Warning: If pain continues more than 10 days, see a doctor.

E

Natural Calcium
500 mg.
100 tablets

SUGGESTED USE:
One tablet three times daily with meals.

One tablet contains 50% of the RDA (Recommended Daily Allowance) for adults and children over 4 years old.

D. Write the letters of the labels *A–E* in the boxes.

1. D

2. ☐

3. ☐

4. ☐

5. ☐

E. **Now find the information in the labels on page 123. Write it on the lines.**

1. What medicine is for the relief of pain from headaches and fever?

   _Buyum Aspirin_____ How many tablets can you take at

   one time? _____ In one day (24 hours)? _____ What should you do

   if you have pain for a long time? _____

2. What medicine is for itching? _____ What's the

   patient's name? _____ Who's his doctor? _____

   How many times a day will the patient take the medicine? _____

   What form is it in (tablets, capsules, liquid, cream, drops)?

   _____ When should he throw it away? _____

3. What can you take as a food supplement? _____ How

   many milligrams are there in one tablet? _____ How many tablets are in

   one container? _____ What does RDA mean? _____

   _____ What percentage of RDA does each tablet contain? _____

4. What cream can you rub on small injuries or sunburn? _____

   _____ What warning is on this (and many other)

   containers? _____

5. What liquid medicine can you take to relieve colds? _____

   _____ How many tablespoons can someone over twelve

   years old take? _____ When? _____ Is the medicine good for

   children? _____

6. How many of the containers have prescription drugs in them?

   _____ How many can you buy over the counter? _____

F. **Bring medicine containers or labels to class. Talk about them.

PART TWO / INFORMATION

● Medical Insurance Plans

Medical Insurance

Basic health insurance covers most costs of hospital care. Major medical insurance covers other costs, like visits to doctors' offices, tests, and the use of equipment. Some plans pay for prescription medicine.

To decide on an insurance plan, you have to find out the answers to these questions: How much and how often do you have to pay for the insurance? How many hospital days will the insurance company pay for? How much will it pay and for what services? How much will you have to pay before the insurance will pay you anything? What expenses won't the company pay for?

Here is an explanation of one kind of student health insurance.

STUDENT ACCIDENT AND SICKNESS INSURANCE PLANS

Plan A is for basic benefits only. Plan B is for basic benefits and major medical.

BASIC BENEFITS (PLANS A AND B)

	Plan A	Plan B
1. Daily Room and Meals in Hospital	$80.00	$115.00
2. Hospital Charges: Operating Room, X-Ray Examinations, Laboratory Tests, Drugs or Medicines UP TO	700.00	80% to 1500.00
3. Emergency Room Charges UP TO	70.00	90.00
4. Surgical Operations	1000.00	1800.00
5. Ambulance Service to and from Hospital	60.00	80.00
6. Visits to Doctor If not in Hospital	20.00	35.00

ACCIDENT AND SICKNESS MAJOR MEDICAL EXPENSE (PLAN B ONLY)

After the first $2000 of payment, the company will pay 80% of the usual and reasonable medical expense up to $25,000.

This policy does not cover any expenses for:

1. injuries from sports

2. eyeglasses or eye examinations

3. pregnancy or childbirth

4. nervous or mental disease

5. dental care or dental X-Rays

A. In the insurance plans on page 125, find the two correct answers to each of these questions. Circle the letters.

1. What kinds of health insurance can students buy?
   a. basic hospital benefits (Plan A)   **c.** a pregnancy plan
   b. a major medical policy (Plan B)   **d.** coverage for dental care

2. How much will the insurance company pay for one day's hospital room and meals?
   a. $80.00 under Plan A   **c.** $115 under Plan B
   b. any amount necessary   **d.** $350 for both plans together

3. What other hospital expenses will Plans A and B pay for?
   a. operating room costs   **c.** drugs or medicines in hospital
   b. eye examinations   **d.** childbirth

4. What expenses won't the insurance cover?
   a. operations (surgery)   **c.** treatment for sports injuries
   b. ambulance service   **d.** nervous disease

B. Fill out this insurance application for yourself. Explain your choices.

APPLICATION FOR STUDENT HEALTH INSURANCE

STUDENT NAME _____ DATE OF BIRTH _____
           last   first   middle

Prices are for one year. Plan A is for basic benefits only. Plan B is major medical insurance.

	Plan A	Plan B
STUDENT ONLY	$300.00 ☐	$380.00 ☐
Student and Husband or Wife	460.00 ☐	580.00 ☐
Student, Husband or Wife, and Children	600.00 ☐	800.00 ☐
Student and Children	440.00 ☐	560.00 ☐

This policy begins only when the STUDENT INSURANCE Company receives this application with full premium payment.

Student's Signature _____ Date _____

**C. Answer these questions: Are the student insurance plans good ones? Why or why not? Do you have or know about any health insurance plans? Tell about them.

PART THREE / SPELLING

● The Consonants *z, s, c, ch, tch, ck, f, ph, gh* ● The *-ing* Ending

Spelling	Examples		
For the "z" sound, use the letter *z* at the beginning of words, and *z* or *s* in other word positions.	zip crazy sneeze	zone dizzy was	buzz disease advise
For the "s" sound, use the letter *c* only before *e, i,* or *y*. Use *s* in all other word positions.	necessary safe loose	cigarettes sick face	messy advice

A. Listen to the sentences. Write the consonant letters.
　　　　z　　s　　c

1. the "z" sound

Bu_z_ _z_ ha_s_ a di__ea__e.

He'__ snee__ing, and hi__

no__e is red.

2. the "s" sound

You don't have a __ickne___, and

no __urgery is ne__e___ary.

Redu__e, and cut out __igarettes.

3. "z" and "s"

You might

lo__e this

loo__e tooth.

4. "z" and "s"

Take my advi__e.

Don't get clo__e to

the patient, and I

advi__e you to

clo__e the door.

5. "z" and "s"

What are tho__e

pri__es? Did you

win a ra__e?

And did you rai__e

your pri__es?

Spelling	Examples	
For the "f" sound, use *f* in most words. Use *ph* in some words and *gh* at the end of a few words.	f̲ill p̲hone lau̲g̲h	safe̲ Ral̲p̲h coug̲h̲

B. Listen to the sentences. Write the consonant letters.

f	Ph	ph	gh

This is Dr. ___ilop's ___armacy ___one. Yes, it's sa___f to___ take a ___ew tablets with ___ood. How are you ___eeling, Ral___? Are you lau___ing or cou___ing?

Spelling	Examples	
For the "ch" sound, use *ch* in most words. Use *tch* after one vowel letter.	c̲hild itc̲h	reac̲h scratc̲h
For the "k" sound, use *k* only before *e*, *i*, or *y*. Use *c* before all other letters. Use *k* after two vowel letters and *ck* after one. Use *ch* in a few words.	k̲eep c̲all weec̲k ac̲h̲e	take̲ c̲ough bac̲k̲ stomac̲h̲

C. Listen to the sentences. Write the consonant letters.

ch	tch

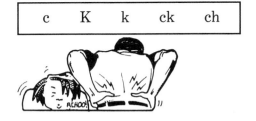

c	K	k	ck	ch

1. His face i___es, and the ___ild shouldn't scra___ his ___eeks or his ___in.

2. Chu___ is si___ with a ___old and a ___ough. ___eith has a ba___a___e. What ___apsules ___an they ta___e?

c	k	ck	ch	tch

3. Are you smo___ing a lot? Do you drink much al___ohol?

Wa___ ___ ___ it, or you ___ould have a heart atta___ ___.

Do your ___ ___ildren need ___ ___e___ ___-ups, too?

<table>
<tr><td></td><td>**Spelling**</td><td>*-ing* Form</td></tr>
</table>

___ ***D.*** **Write other words with the letters *z*, *s*, *c*, *f*, *ph*, *gh*, *ch*, and *k*. Tell the meanings.**

	Spelling	*-ing* Form
write drive	**1.** If a word ends in silent *-e* after a consonant, drop the *-e* and add *-ing*.	writi**ng** drivi**ng**
swim get begin	**2.** If a word or a stressed syllable ends in one consonant after one vowel, double the last consonant and add *-ing*.	swim**ming** get**ting** begin**ning**
sew fix pay	**3.** Don't double *w*, *x*, or *y* at the end of syllables. (*W* and *y* are vowels.)	sewi**ng** fixi**ng** payi**ng**
eat happen	**4.** Add *-ing* to other words.	eati**ng** happeni**ng**

___ ***E.*** **Write the *-ing* words on the lines.**

Last year at this time I was ___enjoying___ life, but I wasn't
            1. enjoy

_____ care of my health. I was _____ several packs
2. take   **3.** smoke

of cigarettes a day and _____ a lot of alcohol. I wasn't
                      4. drink

_____ at all, and I wasn't _____ enough sleep.
5. exercise   **6.** get

But now my friend and I are _____ , _____ ,
                                    7. run   **8.** swim

and _____ tennis several times a week. We're _____
    9. play   **10.** buy

good food and we're _____ it at home. I'm _____
                  11. cook   **12.** cut

out desserts, too. I'm not _____ much weight, but I'm not
                           13. lose

_____ any, either. I'm _____ hard to relax, and
14. gain   **15.** try

I'm _____ to bed early to get more sleep.
   16. go

But I'm _____ terrible these days because I'm not
         17. feel

_____ any fun.
18. have

PART FOUR / READ AND WRITE

● Insurance Claim Forms

Doctors' Statements and Insurance Claim Forms

Some clinics and doctors try to get medical payments directly from insurance companies. Then they bill patients for any additional amount due. Other doctors ask patients to pay them directly. To get money back from their insurance companies, patients fill out claim forms and send them in with doctors' statements.

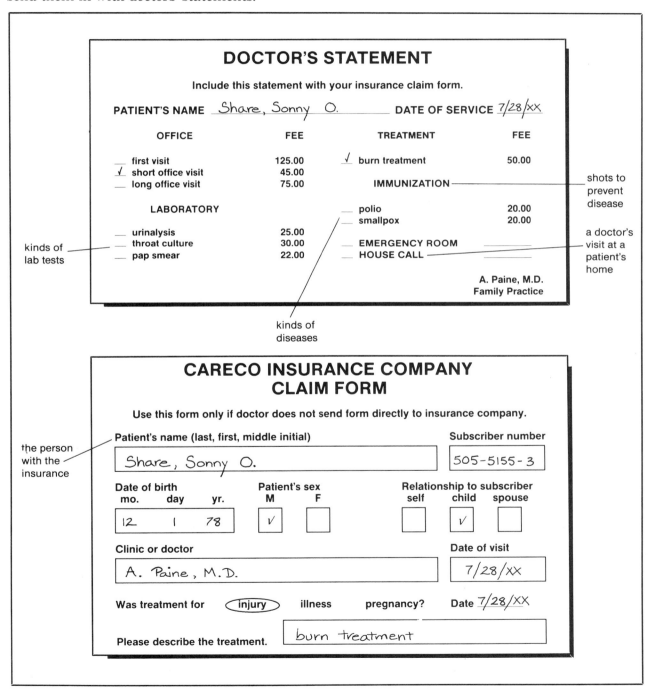

DOCTOR'S STATEMENT

Include this statement with your insurance claim form.

PATIENT'S NAME Share, Sonny O.   DATE OF SERVICE 7/28/xx

OFFICE	FEE
___ first visit	125.00
✓ short office visit	45.00
___ long office visit	75.00

LABORATORY	
___ urinalysis	25.00
___ throat culture	30.00
___ pap smear	22.00

TREATMENT	FEE
✓ burn treatment	50.00

IMMUNIZATION

___ polio	20.00
___ smallpox	20.00
___ EMERGENCY ROOM	_____
___ HOUSE CALL	_____

A. Paine, M.D.
Family Practice

kinds of lab tests

kinds of diseases

shots to prevent disease

a doctor's visit at a patient's home

**CARECO INSURANCE COMPANY
CLAIM FORM**

Use this form only if doctor does not send form directly to insurance company.

Patient's name (last, first, middle initial)

Share, Sonny O.

Subscriber number

505-5155-3

the person with the insurance

Date of birth			Patient's sex		Relationship to subscriber		
mo.	day	yr.	M	F	self	child	spouse
12	1	78	✓			✓	

Clinic or doctor

A. Paine, M.D.

Date of visit

7/28/xx

Was treatment for (injury) illness pregnancy? Date 7/28/xx

Please describe the treatment.   burn treatment

A. Find the information in the forms on page 131. Write it on the lines.

1. What's the patient's name? _Sonny O. Share_ The doctor's name?

_____ The name of the insurance company? _____

2. Is the patient a boy or a girl? _____ How old is he?

_____ Is the health insurance in his name? _____

3. Did the patient have an injury or an illness? _____

What was it? _____

4. What kind of treatment did he get? _____

_____ How much was the total bill? _____

B. Fill out the claim forms for the statements.

DOCTOR'S STATEMENT

Include this statement with your insurance claim form.

PATIENT'S NAME _Klage, Howard G._ DATE OF SERVICE _9/2/xx_

	OFFICE	FEE		TREATMENT	FEE
✓	first visit	125.00	___	burn treatment	50.00
___	short office visit	45.00	___	cyst removal	120.00
___	long office visit	75.00	✓	allergy test	75.00

Dr. Red Rash
Dermatologist

CARECO INSURANCE COMPANY CLAIM FORM

Patient's name (last, first, middle initial)

Clinic or doctor

Date of visit

Please describe the treatment.

DOCTOR'S STATEMENT

Include this statement with your insurance claim form.

PATIENT'S NAME   _Allrite, Gloria_   DATE OF SERVICE _4/11/xx_

LABORATORY		IMMUNIZATION	
✓ blood test	25.00	____ smallpox	20.00
✓ pregnancy test	25.00	____ polio	20.00
✓ urinalysis	25.00		
____ throat culture	30.00	____ EMERGENCY ROOM	_____
____ pap smear	22.00	____ HOUSE CALL	_____

A. Paine, M.D.
Family Practice

GOODCARE INSURANCE COMPANY CLAIM FORM

Patient's name (last, first, middle initial)

Clinic or doctor

Date of visit

Was treatment for   injury   illness   pregnancy?

Please describe the treatment.

C. **Fill out this form with information about yourself or a member of your family from your last or next visit to a clinic or doctor.**

_____ **INSURANCE COMPANY CLAIM FORM**

Patient's name (last, first, middle initial)

Subscriber number

Clinic or doctor

Date of visit

Was treatment for   injury   illness   pregnancy?

Please describe the treatment.

---

*D. **Bring to class clinic, doctors' or medical insurance information and forms. Talk about them.**

CHAPTER
10

The Weekend and Vacations

COMPETENCIES: Getting Information about recreation and entertainment

Using T.V. and radio schedules

Understanding advertisements about movies, concerts, travel, and classes

Reading travel maps and charts

Reading weather maps and reports

Writing postcards

SPELLING: Groups of consonants

GRAMMAR FOCUS: Impersonal *it*

Infinitives after nouns and adjectives

Introduction to clauses

PART ONE / READ AND UNDERSTAND

- Information about Recreation and Entertainment • T.V. and Radio Schedules
- Advertisements about Movies, Concerts, Travel, and Classes

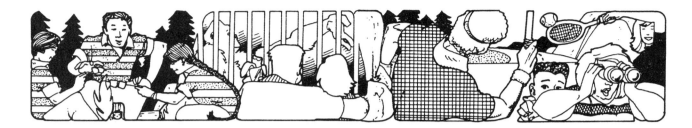

Recreation and Entertainment

Almost everyone has responsibilities—work, school, home and family, the necessities of daily life, etc. Of course it's important to make a living and to take care of responsibilities, but it's also important to have fun. Friends, interests, recreation, and entertainment may be a necessary part of good health.

Some vacation activities can be expensive—hotel stays in big cities, tours, ship cruises, and so on. But it doesn't have to cost a lot to travel. It can be fun to go camping, to visit parks and zoos, to see museums, and to go sightseeing. There may also be places to visit in and near your city or town. Several government and private organizations—the city chamber of commerce, the department of parks and recreation, automobile clubs, travel agencies, etc.— can give you information about places to go and things to do. You can check the telephone book for the addresses and telephone numbers. It's also easy to get information about your city, state or province, and other places to travel from the public library.

Education can be a part of recreation, too. If you enroll in community service classes at local colleges or adult schools, you can learn some new skills, enjoy different kinds of activities, and meet many people with your interests. Class schedules are available from schools by mail and in person, and you can call for information, too.

It's nice to have entertainment in your home—radio, T.V, etc.—and you can entertain yourself in the community, too. Local newspapers usually advertise plays, movies, concerts, sports events, and so on in the calendar section. Most newspapers include a T.V. magazine on weekends and lists of T.V. and radio programs in the daily entertainment sections.

A. Are these sentences true? Write *yes* or *no*.

1. _no_ It's a bad idea to spend time on recreation because you should work and study all the time.

2. _____ It's healthy to enjoy yourself and have fun sometimes.

3. _____ It's always expensive to travel because you have to pay for hotels and a lot of entertainment.

4. _____ If you call public or private organizations and visit libraries, you can get information about recreation and travel.

5. _____ People in the community can take classes in many subjects at local colleges and adult schools.

6. _____ Newspapers usually offer information about entertainment.

B. Write *I* before the places to get information, *V* before the places to visit, and *E* before the different kinds of entertainment.

1. _I_ the chamber of commerce

2. _____ parks and zoos

3. _____ the department of parks and recreation

4. _____ plays and movies

5. _____ museums

6. _____ an automobile club

7. _____ T.V. and radio

8. _____ concerts (music)

9. _____ a travel agency

10. _____ a sports event

11. _____ the public library

12. _____ the local newspaper and telephone book

C. Answer these questions.

1. What do you like to do for fun?

2. Where do you go on the weekends? During vacations?

3. How do you find out about recreation and entertainment in your community?

T.V. and Radio Schedules

Today's Television
7:00 p.m.
2 News—Dan Lather
4 Entertainment Today
5 Family Life—Comedy
11 Movie—*I Remember Papa*
28 The Exercise Show

7:30 p.m.
4 The Price Is Wrong—Game
5 The Alice Show—Comedy
28 Math Education

8:00 p.m.
2 Local News and Weather
4 News Special—Barbara
Waters Talks to the President
28 American Playhouse
Missing Person by Kurt
Kunnicut

What's on Radio?
AM
WABC   790   WFWB   980   WIN   1260

FM
WCRW   89.9   WLOS   93.5   WILD   101.9

Radio Plays
noon   WCRW-FM
Mystery Theater
7:30 p.m.   WLOS
Spanish language

Talk Shows/News
2 p.m.   WABC
Newstalk
4:30 p.m.   WLOS
Car Advice

Music
6 a.m.   WILD-FM
Early Morn Show
6 p.m.   WIN
Dinner Music

Sports
8:15 a.m.   WFWB
Sports news
every hour
12:30 p.m.   WABC
Baseball game

D. Find the information in the schedules. Write it on the lines.

1. The T.V. schedule lists programs for _five_____ channels. The news with

   Dan Lather is on Channel _____ , and the movie *I Remember Papa*

   will be on Channel _____ . Educational shows are on Channel _____ .

2. An exercise show is going to begin at _____ p.m., and there's

   a news special at _____ . At 7:00 on Channel 4, you can see

   _____ .

3. "Family Life" and "The Alice Show" are the names of _____

   shows, and " _____ " is the name of a game

   show. " _____ " is the name of a play.

4. There are _____ AM stations and _____ FM stations on the

   radio schedule. WABC is an _____ station, but WILD is an _____

   station. You can find station WFWB at _____ on the AM dial and

   station WCRW at _____ on the FM dial.

5. There are radio plays on Stations _____ and _____ in the afternoon and evening. Station _____ has programs in Spanish.

6. You can get advice about your car at _____ on Station _____ . WFWB brings you _____ news once an hour, and you can hear a _____ _____ on WABC at 12:30 in the afternoon.

E. **Look at the T.V. and radio schedules in your local newspaper. Talk about the words and the information. Choose programs to watch or listen to.

Ads for Things to Do

BEST PICTURE

LOOK TO THE FUTURE
with Michael Wolf

PG

NOW PLAYING
The Greentree Theater
(818) 555-4560

3:00   6:00   9:00

A

WILLIE NIELSON IN CONCERT
March 21, 22, 23   8:30 p.m.

Tickets now on sale: $22.50/17.00

THE MUSIC HALL   1111 Country Drive
Call **555-8975** to charge tickets

B

LAS VEGAS VACATION!
3 days / 2 nights
Luxury Room
2 Dinners
Musical Show
$59/person
LV RESERVATION SERVICES
Call   1-800-555-7885

C

Beginning Drawing	**Art Smith**
8 Thursdays starting 3/2	7 - 10 p.m.
City High School, Rm. 110	Fee $55

How to Start a Business	**Mel Powers**
1 Saturday: 3/22	9:30 a.m. to 5 p.m.
City College, B Bldg. #222	Fee $30

D

F. **Where is the above information from? Write the letters *A–D* on the lines.**

1. _____ a travel advertisement

2. _____ a list of community service classes and offerings

3. _____ an ad for a musical concert

4. _____ an ad for a movie

G.   Now find the information in the ads. Write it on the lines.

1. The name of the movie in ad A is ___Look to the Future___ ,

   and the star's name is _____ . There are _____ showings

   every day at the _____ Theater.

2. The singer in the concert ad B is _____ . The

   ticket prices are _____ and _____ , and you can call to

   _____ them.

3. The travel ad says you can stay _____ nights in the city of

   _____ _____ . This price includes the hotel room, two

   _____ , and a musical _____ .

4. In the community service program, there are classes in "Beginning _____

   _____ " and "How to Start a _____ ." The

   teacher of the art class is Mr. _____ . It begins in the

   month of _____ and meets for eight _____ at City

   _____ _____ . Mr. Power's business class meets _____

   time on _____ , March _____ , in Room _____ of Building B at

   City College. It begins at _____ a.m. and ends at _____ p.m. It

   costs _____ to take the class.

H.   Look at ads for entertainment in your local newspaper. Talk about the words and the information. Choose events to go to.

PART TWO / INFORMATION

● Road Maps and Charts ● Weather Maps and Reports

Travel Maps and Charts

If you travel by car, it's a good idea to take road maps with you. You can get different kinds of travel maps from bookstores, automobile clubs, travel agencies, gas stations, etc. Most maps include information about mileage (the distance between places).

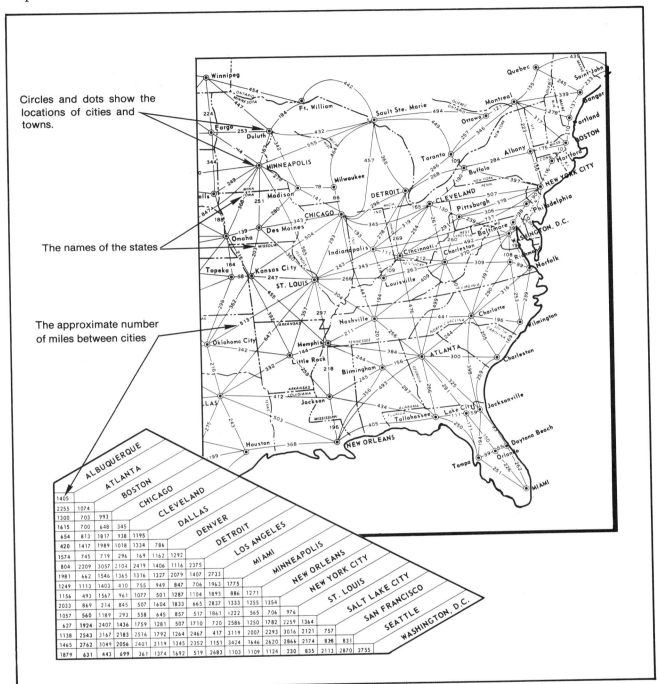

Use the mileage chart to find out the approximate number of miles between two major cities. Then add or subtract the number of miles between cities on the map.

The distance between Chicago, Illinois, and Orlando, Florida

Examples

Chicago to Atlanta (from the chart)	703	OR	Chicago to Miami (from the chart)	1365
Atlanta to Lake City (from the map)	291		Miami to Orlando (from the map)	− 226
Lake City to Orlando (from the map)	+ 150			
TOTAL	1144			1139

A. Use the chart and map on page 141 to figure out those distances. Write them on the lines.

How far is it from

1. Boston, Massachusetts, to Chicago, Illinois? It's ___993___ miles.

2. Cleveland, Ohio, to Minneapolis, Minnesota? It's _____ miles.

3. New York City to New Orleans, Louisiana? It's _____ miles.

4. Washington, D.C., to Kansas City, Missouri? _____ + _____ = _____ miles.

5. Atlanta, Georgia, to Montreal, Canada? _____ + _____ + _____ = _____ miles.

6. St. Louis, Missouri, to Charleston, West Virginia? _____ - _____ = _____ miles.

7. Dallas, Texas, to Albany, New York? _____ - _____ = _____ miles.

B. Choose cities on the map. Figure out the distances between them.

8. It's about _____ miles from _____ to _____ .

9. It's about _____ miles from _____ to _____ .

10. It's about _____ miles from _____ to _____ .

**C. Use road maps to find out the distances between other places.

Road Maps

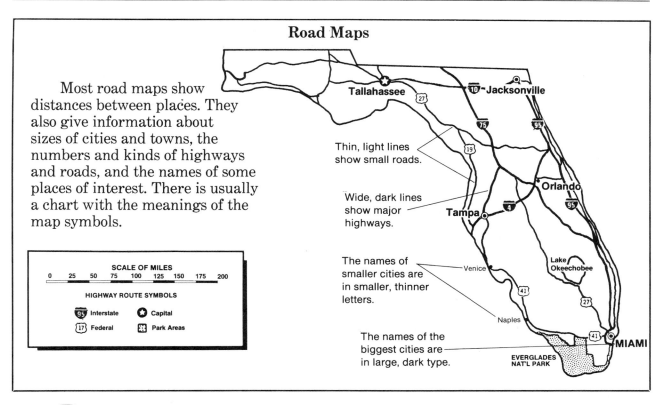

Most road maps show distances between places. They also give information about sizes of cities and towns, the numbers and kinds of highways and roads, and the names of some places of interest. There is usually a chart with the meanings of the map symbols.

SCALE OF MILES

0   25   50   75   100   125   150   175   200

HIGHWAY ROUTE SYMBOLS

95 Interstate   ✪ Capital

17 Federal   ▣ Park Areas

Thin, light lines show small roads.

Wide, dark lines show major highways.

The names of smaller cities are in smaller, thinner letters.

The names of the biggest cities are in large, dark type.

D. **Find the information on the map. Write it on the lines.**

1. This map shows the state of ___Florida___ . The biggest city

   is _____ , and the capital city is _____ . The

   names of two small towns are _____ and _____ . Lake

   _____ and _____ National Park are in the southern

   part of the state.

2. According to the scale of miles, it's about _____ miles from Miami to

   Jacksonville. You can drive on Interstate Highway _____ .

3. To get from Miami to Tampa, you can take Federal Highway _____

   through Naples.

E. **Look at road maps of your state or other states or provinces. What places do you want to visit? Talk about the distances and roads to take to them.

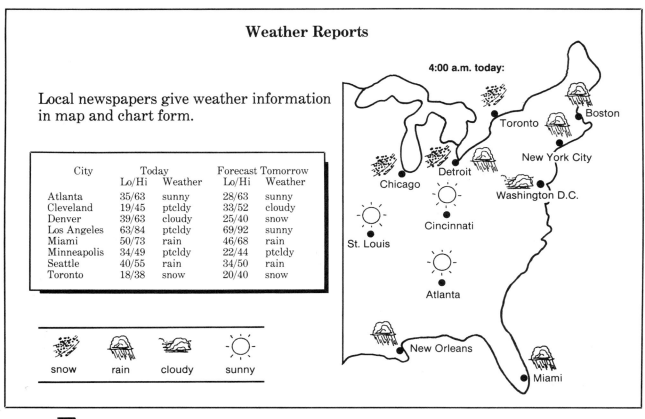

Weather Reports

Local newspapers give weather information in map and chart form.

4:00 a.m. today:

City	Today		Forecast Tomorrow	
	Lo/Hi	Weather	Lo/Hi	Weather
Atlanta	35/63	sunny	28/63	sunny
Cleveland	19/45	ptcldy	33/52	cloudy
Denver	39/63	cloudy	25/40	snow
Los Angeles	63/84	ptcldy	69/92	sunny
Miami	50/73	rain	46/68	rain
Minneapolis	34/49	ptcldy	22/44	ptcldy
Seattle	40/55	rain	34/50	rain
Toronto	18/38	snow	20/40	snow

snow   rain   cloudy   sunny

F. Find the information in the map and chart. Write it on the lines.

1. At 4:00 a.m. today, it was _Snowing_ in Chicago. It was _____

   in Boston and New York City. It was _____ and _____

   in Detroit. It wasn't _____ or _____ in Cincinnati.

2. Today the weather is _____ in Atlanta. There's _____

   in Seattle. It's _____ in Denver and partly _____ in Los

   Angeles. It's _____ in Miami.

3. The lowest temperature in Cleveland today was _____ Fahrenheit.

   It was _____ in Seattle. The temperature will reach a high of

   _____ today in Denver.

4. Tomorrow it's going to be _____ in _____ . It will be

   _____ in _____ . The low temperature in _____ will

   be _____ . The temperature will reach _____ in _____ .

_____**G. **Look at a weather map and chart in today's local newspaper. Tell about the weather today and the weather forecast for your city and other places.**

The Temperature

In most countries, temperature is in degrees Centigrade (Celsius), but in most of North America, weather reports tell the temperature in Fahrenheit. You may want to figure out Fahrenheit temperatures in Centigrade or Centigrade temperatures in Fahrenheit.

To change Fahrenheit degrees to Centigrade, subtract 32. Than multiply by 5/9.

Examples

$$41° \text{ F} - 32 = 9° × 5/9 = 5° \text{ C}$$

$$14° \text{ F} - 32 = -18° × 5/9 = -10° \text{ C}$$

To change Centigrade degrees to Fahrenheit, multiply by 9/5. Then add 32.

Examples

$$15° \text{ C} × 9/5 = 27° + 32 = 59° \text{ F}$$

$$-5° \text{ C} × 9/5 = -9° + 32 = 23° \text{ F}$$

_____H. **Do the math problems.**

1. 41° F = __5__ ° C

2. 32° F = _____° C

3. 59° F = _____° C

4. 23° F = _____° C

5. 95° F = _____° C

6. 0° C = _____° F

7. 10° C = _____° F

8. 20° C = _____° F

9. -5° C = _____° F

10. 35° C = _____° F

_____*I. **Figure out some of the Centigrade temperatures from the chart on page 144.**

PART THREE/ SPELLING

• Groups of Consonants

Many words have two or more consonant sounds together. Here are some examples.

<u>pl</u>aces   <u>sch</u>ool   <u>tr</u>avel   <u>progr</u>am   ca<u>mp</u>ing   i<u>mp</u>ortant

_____ **A.** **Listen to the sentences. Write the letters.**

b	c	d	f	g	h	l	n	p	r	s	t	x

1. Enjoy the sun and sea on a weeke<u>n</u> <u>d</u>

   ___ ___uise! Our ___ ___ice in___ ___udes

   ___ ___eakfa___ ___, lu___ ___ ___, dinner, and our

   re___ ___eation ___ ___o___ ___am. Get ne___ ___ ___

   mo___ ___ ___'s ___ ___ ___edule ___ ___om your

   ___ ___avel age___ ___.

b	c	d	g	h	l	m	n	p	r	s	t	w

2. Take a hea___ ___ ___y vacation in the ___ ___ean

   mountain air. You can ___ ___ay at a ra___ ___ ___

   or in a te___ ___ at a ca___ ___ ___ ___ou___ ___.

   We have sunny weather, but it gets wi___ ___y,

   so ___ ___ing wa___ ___ ___ ___eaters.

_____ ***B.** **Write other words with two or more consonant sounds together. Tell the meanings.**

PART FOUR / READ AND WRITE

- Postcards

A Postcard

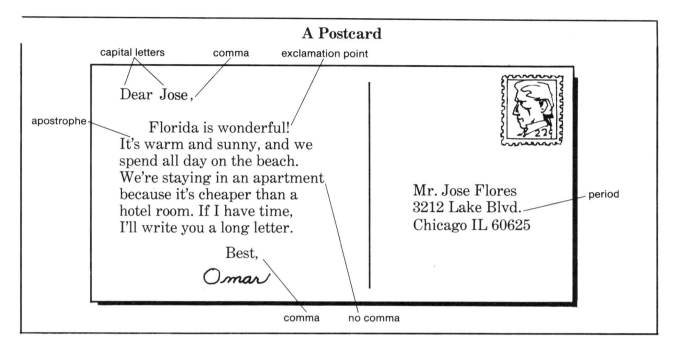

capital letters　　comma　　exclamation point

apostrophe

Dear Jose,

Florida is wonderful!
It's warm and sunny, and we
spend all day on the beach.
We're staying in an apartment
because it's cheaper than a
hotel room. If I have time,
I'll write you a long letter.

Best,

Omar

comma　　no comma

Mr. Jose Flores
3212 Lake Blvd.
Chicago IL 60625

period

A. Change the small letters to capital letters. Write the periods, commas, apostrophes, and exclamation points.

dear haruko

camping is terrible it rained
yesterday so today it s too wet to
take a walk i can t sleep at night
because it s too cold in the tent if
we don t move to a hotel i m going
to get sick i miss you and i can t
wait to get home

love
Debra

ms haruko ito

204 northland st

st louis mo 63130

B. **Cover the words under each line with paper. Listen and write. Then check your writing.**

_____

Dear Paul,

_____

I love big cities!

_____

It's fun to go sightseeing, and we're enjoying the museums.

_____

We know about all the places to visit and things to do

_____

because we're staying with friends.

_____

If I have time, it will be nice to go shopping.

C. Choose a picture and write a postcard. Address it to a friend or relative.

PLACE
STAMP
HERE

**D. Write a postcard to a friend or relative about things to do and see in your city. Or write some postcards on your next vacation trip.